# ENHANCING EMPLOYEE PERFORMANCE

Other books on employee development available from Management Books 2000 Ltd (see page 196):

*Who Cares Wins* (Peter Savage)
*The Green-Fingered Manager* (Roy Bailey)
*Team Management* (Charles Margerison and Dick McCann)
*Dear Boss...* (Trish Nicholson)

# ENHANCING EMPLOYEE PERFORMANCE

**Bernard Katz**

**John Docherty**

2000

First published in 1994 by Management Books 2000 Ltd
125a The Broadway, Didcot, Oxfordshire OX11 8AW

Printed and bound in Great Britain by
BPC Wheatons Ltd, Exeter



British Library Cataloguing in Publication Data is available

ISBN 1-85252-230-5

# PREFACE

Is your company doing well? Is the performance of employees within your company helping it to grow? Business success and organizational efficiency do not just happen, even though the formula for success may seem straightforward: recruit the right people, train them and motivate them.

Reality is frequently difficult because obstacles continuously arise. Customers are offended; deadlines are missed through absenteeism, alcoholism, worker conflict, insufficient staff at peak times, or simply poor training; opportunities are lost; morale is low. Successful companies share all these hurdles with those who struggle, but they meet them positively and go forward.

This book is about achieving success in management. It provides managers with the tools to make staff perceive the right solutions, without precedent or hand-holding. The reader is helped to identify the causes of poor performance, and to apply sound practical solutions within a controlled environment, with or without trade union presence, in which employees give of their best.

The book is in two parts. Part 1 starts the success process by dealing with 'finding' and 'selecting' the right candidate for a cultural fit within the work team. Part 2 develops the managers' skills in creating an added-value employee. There are practical methods for training, for building up strong employee relationships, for getting help from good job design, and for the ever-present requirement of motivating staff to want to work hard.

# CONTENTS

# MATRIX OF TOPIC QUESTIONS

A question and answer format is used throughout the book to help readers identify topics of particular interest. Page references are given below.

# Part 1

# FINDING THE RIGHT EMPLOYEE

# 1

# THE STARTING POINT

Before reading this chapter try to answer the following questions. The material is worked through in the text. Questions and answers appear together at the end of the chapter by way of summary.

## Questions

- What is human resource planning?
- How is a human resource plan prepared?
- How are job descriptions best prepared?
- What procedures are appropriate to monitoring an existing human resource plan?
- What is the significance of labour turnover to human resource planning?
- What information is included in a human resource forecast?
- What is the format of a human resource strategy?

## Setting the Scene
### *Question: What is human resource planning?*

In today's commercial environment a human resource planning strategy is an essential ingredient of corporate success. Human resources, also know as HR, are now the modern buzz words for 'manpower'. The purpose of human resource planning, for an organization of any size, is to help that organization improve its human resource utilization. It is designed to ensure that at any time there are sufficient employees of the right number and quality to create the organization's output of goods and services.

The need to take HR planning seriously is more important than at any time in the past. The cost of hiring and training employees is high; the cost of termination is high; and redundancy payments in excess of the statutory requirement are becoming the norm, whilst increasingly there is the possibility of financial compensation if dismissal is unfair.

There are also other reasons to argue the case for a human resource planning strategy:

- The type of labour required by companies is changing rapidly due to advances in technology.
- Increasing recognition of human attributes is seen as a key ingredient to successful performance.
- The view that there is likely to be a shortage of skilled employees in the future, unless people currently out of the labour market are encouraged to enter and receive appropriate training.

Hand in hand with human resource planning is the requirement to provide training to achieve the necessary skills level to maximize employee resources. The cost of labour is ever increasing, and companies cannot afford to overman or to be undermanned and incur the cost of overtime payments. Similarly, the costs of using subcontracted labour is invariably higher than using own employees. The worst scenario of inadequate HR planning is failure to meet customer orders through lack of employees.

Effective human resource planning reconciles cost with employee requirements in a manner that meets the company's corporate objectives.

## Starting Up

### *Question: How is a human resource plan prepared?*

### *Step 1*

The first step in preparing an HR plan is to carry out an HR inventory in terms of the total numbers employed. It is the process of setting the scene. Personnel are analysed by occupational groups and functions, on a monthly basis over a 12-month period. Any significant change in numbers is identified and the reasons for the change provided.

The information should be completed by each function (see Figure 1.1) and a composite form (Figure 1.2) is used to show total employees. Where appropriate, employee figures are analysed by full-time workers and part-time workers. It is also worth noting any temporary labour or contract staff employed, and the reasons for their engagement: in such circumstances, a question to be asked is: 'Is the engagement of such staff a result of poor human resource planning in the past?'

The fact-finding of the HR inventory is the precursor to the positive actions of employee forecasting and estimating. There is downside too: these aspects of HR planning expose limitations as projections extend into the future. It is sensible to look ahead in time in terms of re-equipment, of apprenticeship, and all the implications of the human resource function, but the further into the future HR plans extend the more subject they are to market, political and environmental forces.

### *Step 2*

The second step in the human resource planning process is to consider in detail each job listed within the organization. A job description should be prepared for each job. The purpose of this is to audit tasks being carried out by job holders in order to ensure all the tasks are actually required and relevant to the achievement of work objectives.

### *Step 3*

An HR policy is established and a plan of action initiated to cover recruitment requirements, training and development of employees, assessment of employee performance and the reduction in employee requirements wherever appropriate.

Function............................................ Month..............................

| Occupation | Actual | Budget | Variance | Last Month | Last Year | Temporary Labour | Subcontract Staff |
|---|---|---|---|---|---|---|---|
| | | | | | | | |

Figure 1.1. Monthly human resource return.

Month........................

| Occupation | Finance | | Production | | Sales | | Marketing | | Technical | | Engineering | | Personnel | | Total | |
|---|---|---|---|---|---|---|---|---|---|---|---|---|---|---|---|---|
| | No. | % | No. | % | No. | % | No. | % | No. | % | No. | % | No. | % | No. | % |
| | | | | | | | | | | | | | | | | |
| Total | | | | | | | | | | | | | | | | |
| Temporary Staff | | | | | | | | | | | | | | | | |
| Subcontract Staff | | | | | | | | | | | | | | | | |
| Grand Total | | | | | | | | | | | | | | | | |

*Figure 1.2. Composite monthly human resource return.*

### *Step 4*
Human resource strategies and tactics are developed to cover recruitment plans, training and development plans, redundancy, succession plans and appraisal.

### *Step 5*
The final stage is the one that is essential to all good plans. It is control and evaluation. Performance is monitored, and contingency resources and planning are available to ensure that what was planned to be workable at the outset remains so.

## Dealing with Basics
### *Question: How are job descriptions best prepared?*

Job descriptions should be prepared by the job holder's manager and job holder. A starting point would be to ask the job holder to write a job description and agree it with his or her manager. It is then approved by a more senior manager to ensure that it fits into the organization's broader goals.

The job holder's manager has to accept responsibility for the completed job description, which must include agreement of the job holder to the job description. This is very important, as it gains commitment to the tasks required to be carried out and establishes the standards of performance expected in each task as the basis on which to review performance.

In preparing job descriptions there are certain essential criteria:

- No overlap of responsibility.
- No duplication of task.
- No key tasks are omitted.

The manager checks job descriptions for his staff and a more senior manager or specialist manager can carry out cross-functional checks. It is also worthwhile to circulate job descriptions amongst the departmental team. This is a further check on duplication, but by far the most important aspect is that each member is made aware of the others' responsibilities and how these interact with their own job.

A key element in preparing the job description is to ask the job holder of any problems which decrease effectiveness. These problems are then discussed fully with the job holder and wherever possible steps taken to resolve them. Very often such problems are easily overcome and the result is improved employee performance.

When undertaking the exercise of preparing a job description it is well worthwhile reviewing the organizational structure to clarify the duties and responsibilities of individuals within the organization. When the exercise is completed, and there are changes in organizational structure, these should be amended on the Monthly Human Resource Returns form (Figure 1.1) and the Composite Monthly Returns form (Figure 1.2). It is recommended that an up-to-date organization chart be prepared.

There are a number of uses of accurate job descriptions for HR planning, numbered on the basis of their increasing importance to enhancing employee performance (No. 5 below is the most important):

1. The job description is important in determining a job grading system, although for job grading other factors must be known too.
2. It provides a basis for establishing training needs so that all job holders are trained to be competent to carry out all the tasks within the job.
3. A job description is essential to the preparation of a person specification. This specification lists the knowledge, skills, aptitudes and personal qualities required by a job holder to perform the job.
4. A basis is provided for a critical survey of organization structure. If the structure is not clearly demarcated, the process of writing the job descriptions is going to highlight problem areas.
5. For the individual the job description sets out what is expected, and on what basis performance is to be measured.

Although all jobs should have a job description, in companies with trade union recognition there may be industrial relations implications. Trade unions may insist that they too are signatories to the job description, and job descriptions may be used to establish demarcation. Resistance can occur when job changes are necessary to meet organizational objectives. Trade unions should always be fully consulted on the need for job descriptions and advised of the positive benefits to be derived from accurate descriptions. Most unions will be fully supportive; but it is unwise to proceed without union agreement, or to proceed with trade union agreement when it is believed that the union has a hidden agenda.

A clear job description is compiled with six distinct steps:

### *Step 1. Identifying the job*

Jobs should be identified by a job title which is a realistic description of the job, not just a grandiose title. How many jobs have the word 'manager' in the title when the job is clearly not in that category?

The function or department in which the job is located must be stated; also the title of the job under which the job holder reports is given so that its level in the hierarchy can be identified.

### *Step 2. Purpose of the job*

This is a brief statement setting out the main purpose of the job indicating how it is different from other jobs. It answers the question, 'Why am I employed?'

### *Step 3. Job content*

The job content is the body of the job description. Headings are given listing the key areas within the job and, when appropriate, with subdivisions to make the job description clear. The process of identifying individual tasks and allocating them to key areas helps to avoid omissions and duplication. The content of the key areas also includes the job holder's activities, both manual and intellectual.

### *Step 4. Standard of performance*

Having identified the activities within the job, it is essential that for each activity a standard of performance is established.

The performance objective should be clearly understandable and measurable both by the job holder and by the organization. It is to this standard of performance that reference is made should the job holder fail to meet the job requirements.

### *Step 5. Conditions of work*

The conditions cover the physical working conditions of the job. Employees who have performed similar jobs in the past may accept existing conditions as normal. Employees new to a job may be surprised at the conditions and if such working conditions have not been brought to their attention at the outset, through the job description, they may well leave the job. (For certain jobs, e.g. office jobs, this section may be omitted from the job description.) This aspect of the job description has a relevance to the preparation of a person specification in respect of physical attributes deemed to be appropriate.

### *Step 6. Additional information*

Sometimes there may be special requirements not listed in the previous sections. These should be identified and listed under this section. Items listed under additional information are of great help in the preparation of a person specification — for example, the job requires a specific skill, using a particular machine, or being able to perform a particularly difficult and complex task.

An example of a job description for a senior secretary is illustrated in Figure 1.3.

---

| | |
|---|---|
| *Job title:* | Senior Secretary |
| *Departments:* | Sales and Marketing |
| *Responsible to:* | Sales and Marketing Director |

*Purpose of the job:*

To provide secretarial services to the Sales and Marketing Department and be responsible for the supervision of other departmental secretaries.

*Job content and standard of performance:*

1 Secretarial duties

1.1 To sort, prioritize and distribute mail to appropriate personnel by mid-morning.

1.2 To provide typing services ensuring:
- all general typing is accurate
- general correspondence is dealt with within 24 hours
- reports and minutes are typed within agreed time limits

1.3 To be responsible for organizing and maintaining accurate diaries for departmental managers.

1.4 To receive all incoming telephone calls, determine reason for each call and redirect to appropriate manager or deal with personally as appropriate and in an efficient and courteous manner.

1.5 To maintain an accurate filing system ensuring all documents for filing are filed within two working days.

1.6 To organize all necessary travel arrangements in accordance with specified requests.

2 Supervisory duties

2.1 To monitor standards of performance of other departmental secretaries and advise job holders of unsatisfactory standards and agree corrective action.

2.2 To provide any necessary training and support to assist secretaries in achieving agreed standards.

2.3 To implement performance appraisal discussions quarterly.

3 Office management

3.1 To be responsible for good office cleanliness by managing subcontracted cleaning agencies and gaining support of staff to good housekeeping practice.

3.2 To ensure building is kept to specified standards by ensuring all necessary work is carried out within building maintenance budget.

4 Personnel administration

4.1 To maintain accurate personnel records and to advise head office personnel department of any personnel changes as and when these occur.

*Additional information:*

(a) To process all departmental orders and invoices daily and forward relevant documentation to head office accounts department.

(b) To be responsible for petty cash float of £700 and to reconcile accounts weekly.

---

*Figure 1.3. Job description for a senior secretary.*

## Making the System Work
### *Question: What procedures are appropriate to monitoring an existing human resource plan?*

To evaluate a human resource plan there are four discrete steps.

1. *Carry out an audit of employees against job descriptions.* A check is made to see which employees are able to perform the job to the level of performance required, and conversely which staff cannot achieve the required levels. For those job holders whose performance is unacceptable additional training has to be provided to upgrade performance. If additional training does not improve performance, the job holder will be considered for redeployment where the qualifications, skills and attributes are best matched against job requirements.

Some may consider that the tasks of preparing accurate job descriptions and the matching of job holder performance against the job description are long and tedious — but they are key elements in enhancing employee performance. The 'right person' must be in the 'right job'. Employee performance is then at its maximum. This is the pathway to meeting corporate goals and satisfying customer requirements.

2. *On a regular basis carry out analyses of employees leaving, by age and by service, and reasons for leaving.* From the results of these analyses labour turnover can be calculated and reasons for leaving determined. This information forms the historical data from which future human resource requirements are projected. In turn, the forecasts permit the formulation of recruitment policies.

3. *Determine the age distribution of the workforce to assess any imbalance in particular functions or occupational groups.* If too many employees of the same age group are in a particular function or occupation, problems may well arise. An example is too many key workers retiring within a short period. Other examples are too many older workers, causing retraining problems, and too many younger workers with lack of experience, resulting in higher labour turnover rates and the likelihood of more errors. The age profile of workers is also a key statistic in determining pension costs.

Figure 1.4 is an illustration of a form used for showing age distribution. The form should be completed for each function as well as for the total organization.

For period ending........................................

| Occupation | 16–20 | | 21–25 | | 26–30 | | 31–35 | | 36–40 | | 41–45 | | 46–50 | | 51–55 | | 56–60 | | 61–65 | | Total | |
|---|---|---|---|---|---|---|---|---|---|---|---|---|---|---|---|---|---|---|---|---|---|---|
| | No. | % | No. | % | No. | % | No. | % | No. | % | No. | % | No. | % | No. | % | No. | % | No. | % | No. | % |
| | | | | | | | | | | | | | | | | | | | | | | |
| Total | | | | | | | | | | | | | | | | | | | | | | |

*Figure 1.4. Age analysis form.*

For period ending........................................

| Occupation | Under 1 year (months) | | | | | | | | | | | Number of years: More than: | | | | | | | | | | | Total |
|---|---|---|---|---|---|---|---|---|---|---|---|---|---|---|---|---|---|---|---|---|---|---|---|
| | 1 | 2 | 3 | 4 | 5 | 6 | 7 | 8 | 9 | 10 | 11 | 1 | 2 | 3 | 4 | 5 | 10 | 15 | 20 | 25 | 30 | 35 | |
| | | | | | | | | | | | | | | | | | | | | | | | |
| Totals | | | | | | | | | | | | | | | | | | | | | | | |

*Figure 1.5. Service analysis form.*

4. *Analyse employees by service so that occupations or functions experiencing labour turnover in the early period of employment can be identified.* Analysis by service will also show how many employees form the hard core of the workforce. This information is useful in improving recruitment practice and helping to reduce labour turnover. The service analysis form (Figure 1.5) can be used for analysing service either by function or by company. A more detailed analysis of early service is shown. After five years employee retention rates are much higher. This information can then be transferred to another, the historical service analysis (Figure 1.6), to show the trend and how it is changing.

| | Percentage of total employees | | | | |
|---|---|---|---|---|---|
| Length of service | 19-- | 19-- | 19-- | 19-- | 19-- |
| Under 1 year | | | | | |
| 1–5 years | | | | | |
| 6–10 years | | | | | |
| 11–15 years | | | | | |
| 16–20 years | | | | | |
| 21–25 years | | | | | |
| 26–30 years | | | | | |
| 31 years + | | | | | |

*Figure 1.6. Historical service analysis form.*

Another useful form, the age and service analysis (Figure 1.7), is used to show age and length of service combined. It provides answers to very important questions: 'Is the age and service profile acceptable?' and 'If the age and service profile is not acceptable, what is desired?'

Monitoring 'actual' against 'what is planned' will demonstrate the relative success of the human resource planning policy. Two examples of policies are: (i) retain more labour to increase years of service and (ii) recruit younger employees in the future to meet projected needs of the business.

| Age in years | Under 1 year | Years of service | | | | | | | | | | | Total |
|---|---|---|---|---|---|---|---|---|---|---|---|---|---|
| | | 1 | 2 | 3 | 4 | 5 | 6–10 | 11–15 | 26–20 | 21–25 | 26–30 | 31+ | |
| 16–20 | | | | | | | | | | | | | |
| 21–25 | | | | | | | | | | | | | |
| 26–30 | | | | | | | | | | | | | |
| 31–35 | | | | | | | | | | | | | |
| 36–40 | | | | | | | | | | | | | |
| 41–45 | | | | | | | | | | | | | |
| 46–50 | | | | | | | | | | | | | |
| 51–55 | | | | | | | | | | | | | |
| 45–60 | | | | | | | | | | | | | |
| 61–65 | | | | | | | | | | | | | |
| Total | | | | | | | | | | | | | |

*Figure 1.7. Age and service analysis form.*

| Period.......................... | | | | | | | |
|---|---|---|---|---|---|---|---|
| Reasons | Finance Nos. | Produc-tion Nos. | Sales Nos. | Marketing Nos. | Technical Nos. | Personnel Nos. | Total |
| *Involuntary*<br>Redundancy | | | | | | | |
| Retirement | | | | | | | |
| Ill health | | | | | | | |
| Death | | | | | | | |
| Unsatisfactory performance | | | | | | | |
| Unsatisfactory conduct | | | | | | | |
| Left district | | | | | | | |
| *Total* | | | | | | | |
| *Voluntary*<br>Transfer to another company | | | | | | | |
| Housing difficulties | | | | | | | |
| Transport problems | | | | | | | |
| Dissatisfaction with superior | | | | | | | |
| Dissatisfaction with other workers | | | | | | | |
| Dissatisfaction with working conditions | | | | | | | |
| Hours of work | | | | | | | |
| Pay rates | | | | | | | |
| *Grand total* | | | | | | | |

*Figure 1.8. Leavers' analysis form.*

## An Important Factor

### *Question: What is the significance of labour turnover to human resource planning?*

Labour turnover is a vital inbuilt control factor of HR planning. Together with the reasons for terminations, i.e. voluntary or involuntary, labour turnover is an indicator of morale within the organization.

Finding out why staff leave when the terminations are voluntary must be an automatic procedure for an organization. An interview by a senior person should probe to establish the real reason for leaving, which may not be the first reason given. This interview is best conducted by a person other than the employee's immediate superior, who may be the cause of the employee leaving. Several staff leaving the same department suggests a manager-subordinate relationship problem.

Some labour turnover is inevitable, and may indeed be advantageous to a company in minimizing planned redundancies. Such situations also open up opportunities for promotion. An organization needs to determine what level of turnover is acceptable, and what should and could be avoided. Voluntary terminations must be examined by function, department, occupation, age and service to see whether there are unsatisfactory areas. Remedial action is then possible in these areas. Figure 1.8 illustrates a form designed to analyse reasons for leaving.

There is a useful formula to measure labour turnover. This is the *turnover rate,* and is calculated by adding the number of leavers over a period of time and expressing it as a percentage of the average number employed during the same period:

$$\text{Turnover rate} = \frac{\text{Number of leavers in specified period}}{\text{Average number employed in same period}} \times 100$$

This formula can be used at functional, occupation or company level, and is calculated for any appropriate period, i.e. monthly, quarterly or annually. It is useful to make comparisons against the previous similar periods, noting the trends so that action can be taken. A weakness in the labour turnover rate is that it includes all leavers and does not distinguish between those with different lengths of service. Short-service employees are more likely to leave than long-term employees. To overcome this problem there is another measurement called the *stability index.* This gives the number of employees with more than one year's service divided by the number of employees a year ago:

$$\text{Stability index} = \frac{\text{No. of employees with more than 1 year's service}}{\text{No. of employees 1 year ago}}$$

A comparison between the two figures shows whether the problem of turnover is among new recruits or among longer service employees, or both.

## Being Practical

### *Question: What information is included in a human resource forecast?*

Forecasting HR requirements is complex. Methods of forecasting vary from industry to industry and from company to company. The common theme of all HR forecasts is that they relate closely to specified sales or production targets and the employee implications have to be examined before the targets are agreed.

Companies must take into account a number of factors in the preparation of an HR forecast:

- Past employment trends.
- The results of work study.
- The results of O. & M. studies.
- Increases in labour productivity.
- Informed opinions of experienced managers.

Forecasts should be both short-term, i.e. less than one year, and long-term, i.e. up to three years (see Figure 1.9). It is recommended that such human resource returns are reviewed each quarter, particularly in relation to the short-term forecast.

## The Right Shape

### *Question: What is the format of a human resource strategy?*

The starting point for an HR strategy is a employee forecast and current historical employee statistics. The strategy is specific to the data and develops in logical sequence, from the answers to the following questions:

Function.......................... Month..........................

| Occupation | Actual | Budget | Variance | Last Month | Last Year | Temporary Labour | Subcontract Staff |
|---|---|---|---|---|---|---|---|
| | | | | | | | |

*Figure 1.9. Monthly human resource return.*

*If the forecast is for an increase in labour —*

- What type of labour is required?
- When is the labour required?
- Given the labour turnover rates, how many employees need to be recruited?
- What is the desired age profile?
- How many positions can be filled by internal candidates?
- What training is needed?

*If the forecast is for a reduction in labour —*

- What is the projected number of staff to be shed?
- Over what period of time is the forecast valid?
- Given the turnover rates, will natural wastage prevent the need for redundancies?
- If redundancies are inevitable, what are the legal implications pertaining to consultation period and to varying periods of statutory notice?
- What selection methods are to be employed?
- What are the implications of 'last in, first out'? Companies who operate on 'last in, first out' may be left with a much higher age and service profile that can cause problems in later years.
- Is early retirement an option? Attractive redundancy payments can entice older employees and longer-service employees to accept redundancy.

In whatever selection process is adopted, the company must ensure it retains within the business sufficient employees with the required abilities to meet the corporate objectives. It is quite normal for the human resource forecast to show increases in numbers for certain groups of workers and decreases for others.

A human resource strategy allows companies to be proactive, not reactive. Constant hiring and firing of staff is costly, bad for employee morale and does little for customer satisfaction. Companies that prepare an HR strategy show that they see their employees as a vital resource, as important, if not more so, than finance. Most companies, certainly the successful ones, prepare a business plan detailing profit forecast, capital spend, cashflow, debtors, creditors, return on assets, etc. Many if not all of these companies stress the importance of their human resources to their business. But the experience of the authors suggests a much smaller number prepare a human resource plan — certainly far fewer than those who prepare a business or financial plan.

This chapter argues that HR planning is an essential ingredient of successful company performance and customer satisfaction.

## Summary

*Question:* What is human resource planning?
*Answer:* HR planning is a planned strategy to make the best possible use of all personnel working in an organization. It is designed to ensure that at all times there are sufficient employees of the right number and quality to generate the organization's projected output of goods and services.

*Question:* How is an HR plan prepared?
*Answer:* There are five steps in the preparation of an HR plan:

Step 1 Carry out an employee inventory, analysing by occupational groups and functions over set periods of time.
Step 2 Analyse every job within the organization through the preparation of a job description.
Step 3 Establish an HR policy and plan of action.
Step 4 Develop human resource strategies and tactics.
Step 5 Control and evaluation.

*Question:* How are job descriptions best prepared?
*Answer:* The preparation of a job description begins with the perception of the job holder and achieving agreement on form and content with the immediate superior. Responsibility for the job description rests with the job holder's manager. There are six steps:

Step 1 Identifying the job.
Step 2 Purpose of the job.
Step 3 Job content.
Step 4 Standard of performance.
Step 5 Conditions of work.
Step 6 Additional information.

*Question:* What procedures are appropriate to monitoring an existing human resource plan?
*Answer:* There are four discrete steps in monitoring an existing plan:

Step 1 Carry out an audit of employees against job descriptions.
Step 2 Regularly analyse employees leaving by reasons of age and service.
Step 3 Monitor age distribution to identify areas of imbalance.
Step 4 Monitor distribution by service to identify the numbers retained within the hard core of the workforce.

*Question:* What is the significance of labour turnover to HR planning?
*Answer:* Labour turnover is a control factor of human resource planning. It measures leavers, allowing comparisons to be made, trends to be identified, and the opportunity to investigate any adverse patterns arising.

*Question:* From what information is a human resource forecast developed?
*Answer:* An HR forecast is built up from:

- Past employment trends.
- The results of work study.
- The results of O.& M. studies.
- Increases in productivity.
- Informed opinions of experienced managers.

*Question:* What is the format of a human resource strategy?
*Answer:* A human resource strategy starts from an employee forecast and historical HR statistics and proceeds to answer 'How?', 'When?' and 'What?' questions relating to human resource use.

# 2

# RECRUITING THE RIGHT EMPLOYEE

Before reading this chapter answer the following questions. The material is worked through in the text. Questions and answers appear together at the end of the chapter to form a summary.

## Questions

- What are the preparatory stages of the recruitment process?
- When recruiting internally, where does the recruitment process begin?
- What advertising options are available when recruiting personnel externally?
- What is the format of a successful recruitment advertisement?
- What are the guidelines for selecting a recruitment agency?

## Preliminary Ways

***Question: What are the preparatory stages of the recruitment process?***

In the structured climate of human resource planning, records should be kept of recruitment activities. Expenditure has to be allocated to a labour costs budget, and it is helpful to keep details of the authorization for the personnel that are to be recruited. Some companies are careless about the way in which requests for replacement or additional staff are made. Possibilities of subsequent dispute or recrimination can be avoided by the completion of a staff requisition form. This is the first stage in the recruitment process.

The cost of labour is expensive, and the recruitment of staff should only be approved by senior personnel. Questions to be asked, before approval is given are:

- If I do not fill this position, what is the effect on the company?
- Are the duties and responsibilities of the projected post of a permanent nature?
- Can the duties and responsibilities of this post be allocated to another position or shared between other posts?
- Can the appointment be filled by a temporary employee?

When the only solution is the employment of additional staff, authorization is given. The information on a staff requisition form will include:

1. Name and identification of originating department
2. Job title
3. Main job function
4. Salary
5. Grade
6. Reason for requisition
   (a) replacement
   (b) new appointment
   (c) temporary appointment
7. Date required by
8. Signature of authorizing manager
9. Date

The second step in recruiting the right employee is the preparation of a person specification. The person specification describes the personal skills and attributes required by the ideal candidate. Irrespective of the level of the appointment, the person specification is best constructed under five main headings:

### *1. Qualifications/knowledge*

Under this heading are listed the qualifications and/or knowledge required by the job holder. It is important that these are relevant to the job in question, irrespective of whether the employee is asked to undertake other tasks from time to time.

### *2. Skills, abilities and aptitudes*

The specific skills, abilities and aptitudes required as necessary for successful performance in the job.

### *3. Experience required*

Often, this is the most important element within the specification. This section must describe accurately the hands-on experience needed by the applicant to meet the demands of the job.

### *4. Behavioural attributes*

Management is becoming increasingly aware of the importance of the behavioural area. The human attributes or personality of a candidate are in many cases critical to successful performance in the job, particularly when an employee is required to be part of a team or when the job involves customer contact.

### *5. Physical attributes*

Great care is needed in describing the physical qualities required by the job holder. Discrimination is a sensitive issue and must be avoided.

When writing a person specification it is useful to consider each of the above items on the two levels of (a) essential characteristics and (b) desirable characteristics.

An example of a person specification (Figure 2.1) is given for the senior secretary of the job description illustrated in Chapter 1.

## Using In-house Resources

### *Question: When recruiting internally, where does the recruitment process begin?*

Looking within the company is the starting point to finding an employee to fit the person specification. Clearly there is a mutual advantage in finding an existing employee whose contribution to the company would be greater in the new position. Such employees can be found by reference to a company succession plan, which is part of the human resource planning process.

1. *Qualifications/knowledge*

| | |
|---|---|
| Essential: | GCSE academic standard including English and Maths. |
| | Typing 50 wpm; shorthand 100 wpm |
| | Use of word processor |
| Desirable: | Book-keeping knowledge |

2. *Skills, abilities and aptitudes*

| | |
|---|---|
| Essential: | Ability to supervise staff |
| | To use own initiative |
| | Schedule work arrangements for superiors |
| Desirable: | Interviewing and training skills |

3. *Experience required*

| | |
|---|---|
| Essential: | 5 years' secretarial experience in commercial environment |
| Desirable: | Previous supervisory experience |
| | WordPerfect |

4. *Behavioural attributes*

| | |
|---|---|
| Essential: | Affiliative and socially confident |
| | Conscientious |
| | Dependable |
| | Energetic |
| Desirable: | Sympathetic, ambitious, flexible |

5. *Physical attributes:*

| | |
|---|---|
| Essential: | Good verbal communication skills |
| | Neat and tidy in appearance |
| Desirable: | Non-smoker |

*Figure 2.1. Person specification for senior secretary.*

For each position within the company covered by the plan, employees are identified who are currently capable of carrying out the work, or who have the potential to do the job in question.

Alternatively, the position may be advertised within the company. Applicants who apply should be subjected to the same selection process as external candidates. Any temptation to relax or reduce the selection criteria because the candidate is known has to be resisted. Interviewers should be aware that there may be discrimination against internal candidates, on the basis that the employer knows much more about them. Would external candidates be appointed if the same knowledge of the applicant was known?

Another process is to establish a transfer register. Employees who wish to transfer to other jobs internally will submit a transfer request. The employee is then interviewed by his manager and/or the personnel manager as to suitability for other positions within the company. This method speeds up the process of internal selection. It is also valuable in identifying problem areas where significant numbers of employees want a transfer from a particular job or section.

Not long ago an Application for Transfer Register was introduced into a company in which one of the authors was working. Within two weeks of the introduction of the system, about 10 per cent of the workforce registered for a transfer, but the numbers included 100 per cent of one department. The company had been aware of some discontent in this department but had done nothing. They were immediately shocked into positive action by the transfer requests. Subsequently, 80 per cent of the employees withdrew their applications. All of the employees who applied for transfer were interviewed to establish the reason for their requests for a transfer. The reason most gave was a desire to move to a job with better pay, or a job perceived as having better job satisfaction. After 12 months approximately one third had been transferred, many on a job swap arrangement. During the year labour turnover reduced by 25 per cent. Trade union representatives and supervisors agreed that the system was beneficial to both employees and management.

At all levels within the organization every effort should be made to fill vacancies internally. But care is essential in the recruitment process to see that internal candidates meet the person specification and are capable of performing the job to a satisfactory standard. There are valuable spin-offs from making internal appointments. Employee morale is increased, job satisfaction is increased, and both lead to better employee performance. In addition, a reputation for employee development is created or enhanced, which also makes the task of external selection easier.

## Opportunity Knocks

***Question: What advertising options are available when recruiting personnel externally?***

When the company is unable to fill a position internally it must decide how it can recruit in the most effective way. There are two major options:

- The company itself advertises for staff, undertaking its own recruitment and selection programme.
- A recruitment agency is invited to take over the recruitment process.

The options are not mutually exclusive, and there are advantages and disadvantages to each. The company may not have the resources and experience to deal with vacancies arising, or it may have advertised to fill vacancies without success and urgently needs help — some recruitment agencies have specific industry expertise and carry a data bank of candidates.

Sometimes both options are taken and agency skills are used in parallel to reinforce the recruitment efforts of the company. A distinction must be drawn between crisis action suggested above and a planned sharing of the recruitment load. But the decision on the recruitment approach is a function of the resources within the company and the cost of filling the vacancy. Unless there are exceptional circumstances 'least cost' is usually required, and the selection process is invariably constrained by specified time limitations.

There are a number of advertising possibilities:

### *Word of mouth*

This is 'no-cost' advertising. Usually it spreads as a knock-on effect from internal advertising. Employees are made aware of a vacancy, and pass this information to family members and friends.

### *Job Centres*

Job Centres of the government's Employment Department service advertise employment vacancies and refer potential recruits at no cost to the employer. In many cases likely recruits registered with the Centre are immediately available.

### *Schools, colleges and universities*

Where potential applicants are likely to be currently in education, employee vacancies are normally advertised free or at very low cost.

Arrangements can usually be made for candidates to be interviewed in situ, if this is desired. Regular contact with educational career departments is recommended.

***Newsagents' windows and advertisement boards***
Newsagents offer an inexpensive method of advertising. This medium is particularly appropriate for low-level positions, or part-time work, where potential employees live near to the company premises.

***Local press or radio***
Local press is perhaps the most frequently used medium for recruitment advertising. It has the ability to reach large numbers of people within the locality and the cost is relatively low. From time to time frequent advertisers can secure editorial publicity without cost.

***National newspapers***
The cost of advertising in the national press is high, restricting the applications sought to more senior positions, but the response generated can be large.

***Trade and professional publications***
Advertising in this medium has the benefit of targeting the right group of potential applicants. Often it is less costly than the national press.

***Cinema***
Cinema attendances are rising but it is unlikely that they will reach the peaks of the 1960s and 1970s. Current audiences are young, and can be appropriate recruitment targets of local employers.

***Leaflet distribution***
Several national and local agencies provide drop-card services. Particularly in housing estates and areas of high-density population.

***HM Forces***
A good source of skilled personnel is to be found among retiring servicemen. Approaches should be made to the nearest outplacement section of HM Forces.

***Company external vacancy board***
A notice board set up at a perimeter fence will be seen by many if the premises border a major road.

### *Other employers*

In recessionary times, advising local non-competitive employers of a company's specific staffing needs may prove mutually beneficial. Companies are invariably glad to introduce outplacement work to employees they are making redundant.

### *Previous applicants*

A company register should be maintained of unsuccessful applicants meeting the requirements of the job, but failing simply because of the competition. A subsequent offer of employment is often accepted.

### *'Milk-round'*

The travelling 'milk-round' for graduate employment is now well established. Each year companies regularly set up a programme of publicity and recruitment at universities and colleges around the United Kingdom. Some universities conduct their own international 'milk-round' programmes, regularly seeking undergraduate and post-graduate students from South-East Asia, Europe, Africa and the USA.

## Winning Ways

### *Question: What is the format of a successful recruitment advertisement?*

An advertisement has to be good to attract candidates that are right for the company. What is good? Historical records culled and filed from appropriate media are helpful in providing information on the style, wording, position, size and cost of advertisements that have proved successful in the past. Further help can be gained from competitors' advertisements that appear frequently. Good advertisements, in practical terms, are advertisements that generate enquiry and response. For national advertising, it is usually best to seek the advice of an advertising agency. Their marketing skills are specialized and they can be expected to have greater in-depth experience than that available in-house.

In a competitive environment it is more important than ever that employers target the right audiences in the most winning ways. Only then are the 'best' employees reached through cost-effective campaigns with little misdirected effort. It is a tall order. How do advertising agencies succeed?

One incentive is from recruitment industry awards, set up to recognize and reward those companies and advertising agencies considered to have produced the best recruitment advertisement in the industry over the past year. There are two major national awards schemes:

1. The IPA, IPM Recruitment Industry Awards sponsored by Personnel Management and *The Daily Express.* 1993 was its thirteenth year.
2. The British Recruitment Advertising Awards sponsored by *Personnel Today* and *The Independent.* 1993 was its fifth year.

The national awards scheme incorporates various categories of recruitment advertising, covering regional, national and trade press advertising as well as posters and brochures.

More than 300 advertisements are entered each year. The standards are high and much creative effort, time and money is spent on the advertisements. Three winning examples from 1993 are illustrated on the following pages.

Fundamental to successful recruitment advertising is the targeting of the audience. Who are the readers that the advertisement is to reach? When the audience is defined, the different costs involved in reaching that audience must be identified. Cost factors must be balanced against readership numbers and the reader profile. For many advertisements impact is partly wasted because the audience, of necessity, has a wide spectrum of interests. For some readers, the advertisement content is of little interest, so the advertising message is very important. Size, frequency and dates of insertion, and position in the advertising medium are important too. The advertisement has to 'sell' its wares in competition with all the other advertisements. Eye-catching advertisements invariably are better than modest advertisements.

*Figure 2.2. 1993 – 'We haven't mentioned the bit about saving lives.' Outright winner of 'Advertisement of the Year' award and winner of 'Best School Leaver/Graduate' category. London Fire and Civil Defence Authority. The advertising agency is Austin Knight.*

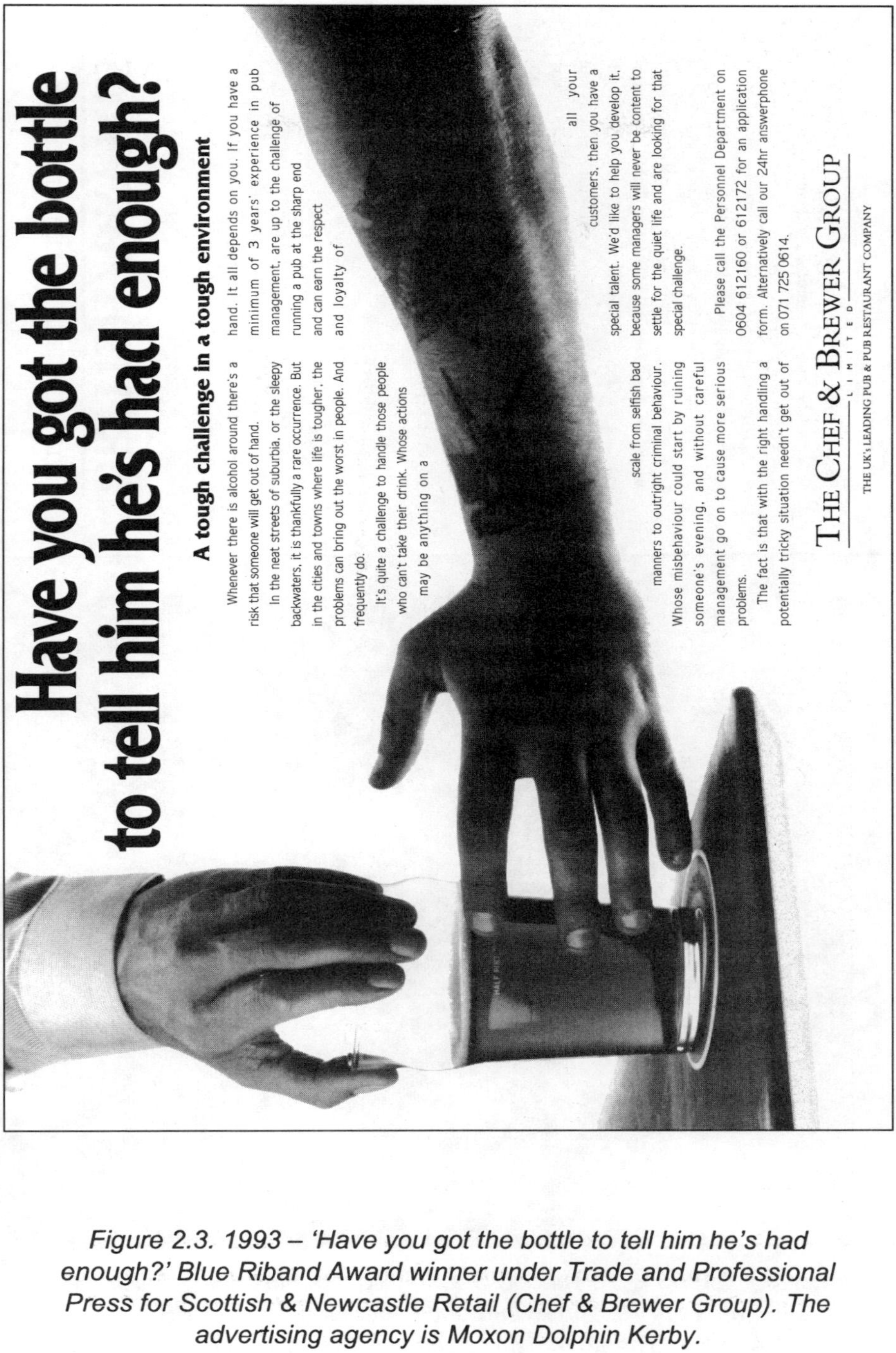


*Figure 2.3. 1993 – 'Have you got the bottle to tell him he's had enough?' Blue Riband Award winner under Trade and Professional Press for Scottish & Newcastle Retail (Chef & Brewer Group). The advertising agency is Moxon Dolphin Kerby.*

*Figure 2.4. 1993 – 'Telephone Sales – "To the ends of the Earth" he told her.' Blue Riband Award under Regional Press for British Airways. The advertising agency is Macmillan Davies.*

There are certain guidelines for achieving a 'good' recruitment advertisement:

- The company name and, particularly, the company logo (if there is one) should appear prominently, to make the advertisement stand out. If the company is not well known, or display of the logo involves high artwork costs, then prominence can be gained by emphasis on the nature of the particular vacancy.
- The position to be advertised must be clearly identified within the advertisement. The top is the best place. An indication of the salary or remuneration package should follow. But if career opportunity, or locality, or job interest are considered to have special importance, then these items should be highlighted instead, or as well.
- The first paragraph gives succinct information about the position and the company that is additional to the information already provided in the wording of the 'available position'.
- A second paragraph accurately and concisely sets out what is required of the job holder. The information is obtained from the job description.
- The qualifications and experience required are stated. This information is taken from the person specification.
- Finally, information is given to the candidate as to how application is to be made and the name and status of the person to whom the application should be addressed.

A successful response rate to advertisements will often depend on how applicants have to apply. For shop-floor personnel, applications in person are usually the best option. Candidates apply, are interviewed, and if successful employed. Many people with little formal education are apprehensive of paperwork. Application forms with many questions are daunting, especially if there are questions relating to skills and experience applicants are unlikely to have.

If the company decides that every applicant should complete an application form, a telephone number should be given and would-be applicants instructed to call that number to request the form. In this way records of the initial response to an advertisement are easily built up. If a curriculum vitae is required, it can be submitted directly by the applicant.

Opinion is divided on the effectiveness of using a CV or a completed company application form. One advantage of using the application form is that all applicants are asked to respond to the same questions. Comparison of the responses obtained is made easier. A valuable point is that the application itself forms the basis for interview discussion.

A disadvantage of using an application form is that different formats are needed for different levels within the organization. At the very least two kinds of application forms are required: one for shop-floor, clerical and administrative positions; another for supervisory and management posts.

If the recruitment advertisement asks candidates to submit a CV then there should be an indication to the candidate of what is to be included. For example, candidates may be asked to state their qualifications, experience, and how their previous work history compares with the job requirements contained within the advertisement. Experience suggests that CVs should be restricted to senior appointments, giving the candidate freedom to determine the style of CV and so influence the potential employer. It is not unknown for companies to request a CV and then to respond to candidates by asking them to complete the company's standard application form.

| Position.................................................. | | | |
|---|---|---|---|
| Media used | | | |
| Size of advert | | | |
| No. of advert insertions | | | |
| No. of replies | | | |
| Number shortlisted | | | |
| Number appointed | | | |
| Cost (£): | | | |
| Cost per reply | | | |
| Date | | | |

*Figure 2.5. Advertisement response analysis form.*

When many positions are advertised and considerable sums are spent on advertisements it is essential to identify cost-effectiveness. A record should be maintained to monitor cost and response. Figure 2.5 illustrates an advertisement response analysis form.

## Do This: Do That

### *Question: What are the guidelines for selecting a recruitment agency?*

There is no shortage of agencies; a single display advertisement usually generates rapid responses from agencies prospecting for new clients to help. Alternatively, names of recruitment agencies are readily found in *Yellow Pages* and in the classified advertisement sections of the press. Although there is certain overlap, agencies operate at three levels:

*Commercial employment agencies.* These include a number of large multiple agencies, with branches in every major town, specializing in particular areas of commerce or the professions. Examples of these agencies are found in accountancy, computing, law and in secretarial services.

*Recruitment consultants.* These organizations provide companies with a varying spectrum of services within the recruitment process. One particularly valuable service is to act as a letterbox: replies to advertisements are sent to the consultants and not to the advertiser, so maintaining anonymity for the advertiser.

*Executive search agencies.* A more popular name for these is 'headhunters'. They are briefed to locate candidates for very senior management positions. In the majority of cases the candidates will currently be working in other organizations.

To help in deciding on the recruitment approach the following guidelines will prove useful:

- Ask whether the recruitment organization can provide an efficient, cost-effective service guaranteed to prove more successful than your own recruitment efforts.
- Endeavour to choose a recruitment agency recommended by satisfied clients. If none is known, ask the agency for a few of their clients to contact.

- Look for an agency advertising vacancies similar to those you require, in the local, national or trade papers.
- Establish the range of tasks the agency is able to perform. For senior appointments you may want them to:

  Assist in preparing job descriptions and job specifications.
  Write advertising copy.
  Advise on and justify placing advertisements in suitable media.
  Interview candidates and subsequently submit a shortlist with written-up interview notes, for final selection.

- Establish the experience the agency has with your industry or profession.
- Establish the fees charged by the agency and the precise services provided for that fee.
- Agree the timescale by which candidates will be available for final selection.

## Summary

*Question:* What are the preparatory stages of the recruitment process?
*Answer:* Initially, confirm that there is no option but to recruit. A staff requisition form is then completed. Finally, a person specification for the vacant post is prepared to match the job description of the post.

*Question:* When recruiting internally, where does the recruitment process begin?
*Answer:* Reference to a company succession plan is the starting point for recruiting internally. Options to follow are (a) advertising within the company and (b) making an application to a transfer register.

*Question:* What advertising options are available when recruiting personnel externally?
*Answer:* Companies must decide whether to manage recruitment advertisement in-house or to employ a recruitment agency, or in certain circumstances to pursue both activities. Candidates will be found through (a) word of mouth, (b) Job Centres, (c) schools, colleges and universities, (d) newsagents' boards, (e) local press and radio, (f) national

newspapers, (g) trade and professional publications, (h) cinema advertising, (i) leaflet distribution, (j) HM Forces, (k) company external vacancy boards, (l) other employees, (m) previous applicants and (n) 'milk-rounds'.

*Question:* What is the format of a successful recruitment advertisement?

*Answer:* Recruitment advertising has the most chance of success when it targets the correctly defined audience. Advertisements should display the company name and logo and clearly describe the position to be filled. They must state what is required of the job holder, the qualifications necessary, and how and to whom the candidate should respond.

*Question:* What are the guidelines for selecting a recruitment agency?

*Answer:* The ideal criteria are recommendations from satisfied clients. Competency in industry specific fields must be established. The range of tasks the agency is to be instructed to perform, cost and the timescale should be agreed in advance.

# 3

# SELECTION

Before reading this chapter answer the following questions to test what you know about the selection process. Give your answers quickly. Do not think for a long time. The questions are repeated at the end of the chapter, together with the answers, as a form of summary.

## Questions

- What routine tasks precede the selection interview?
- How important is testing to the skilled interviewer?
- What interview preparations are critical to success?
- How do good interviewers conduct their interviews?
- What are the salient points of the offer of employment?

## Foundations

***Question: What routine tasks precede the selection interview?***

The candidates' applications have been received and decisions must now be made on who proceeds to an interview and who is rejected. The applications are screened by comparing the person specification

Dear Mr/Mrs ...

With reference to your recent application for employment we invite you to attend for an interview on ...(date) at...(time). On arrival please ask for my secretary, Ms Carol Ward.

It is anticipated that the interview will last about 1½ hours. We shall be using a number of selection tests to help us in our decision-making. Please bring along with you any documentary evidence you may have to support your application, in respect of qualifications, skills and abilities.

Travelling expenses equivalent to the cost of petrol or standard-class public transport fare will be reimbursed at the interview.

Would you please telephone Ms Ward to confirm this appointment or, if the time is inconvenient, to arrange an alternative appointment.

I look forward to meeting you.

Yours sincerely

John B. Heathcoate
PERSONNEL MANAGER

*Figure 3.1. A standard appointment letter.*

against the candidate's application form or CV. (Internal applicants should complete an application form too.) When there appears to be a good match the applicants are listed for interview. A standard letter can be sent (see Figure 3.1). This tells applicants the date and time of the interview, where it is being held, how long the interview is likely to last, the basis for payment of travel expenses and the name of the person to ask for on arrival.

Those who have not been chosen for interview are grouped in a 'rejection' pile and notified in writing. A standard letter can also be used (see Figure 3.2).

> Dear Miss ...
>
> With reference to your recent application for employment by this Company, we regret to inform you that in this instance you have not been successful. The reason is that our job requirements do not meet with your qualifications and experience.
>
> We thank you for giving us the opportunity to consider your application, and wish you every success in finding suitable employment.
>
> Yours sincerely
>
> J.B. Heathcoate
> PERSONNEL MANAGER

*Figure 3.2. A standard rejection letter.*

In a number of cases there will be applications that do not fall easily into the two groups of 'interview' and 'rejection', but are borderline. A third group of 'possibles' is therefore created, and for the moment these are set aside. Depending on the level of success achieved from the 'interview' group, the best of those within the 'possibles' can be called forward for interview or written to requesting specific additional information that may enhance their particular application. Some of the 'possibles' will still be left. These are finally sent a letter of rejection.

A particularly helpful document to use in the selection interview is an interview assessment form (Figure 3.3). A few details are filled in prior to the interview. Salient information from the candidate's appli-

Position: ....................................... Assessor: .......................................

| Person Specification | Application Form/CV | Selection Test | Interview | Reference Documents |
|---|---|---|---|---|
| Qualifications Knowledge | | | | |
| Skills Abilities | | | | |
| Experience required | | | | |
| Behavioural attributes | | | | |
| Physical attributes | | | | |

Overall assessment – tick as appropriate:

....More than meets requirements ....Meets requirements ....Lacking in some requirements ....Not suitable

*Figure 3.3. An interview assessment form.*

cation that matches the requirements of the person specification is written on the document in advance, so that it can be ticked, or scored out, or amended during the interview. When selection tests are used, the test results and the name of the test are entered too.

Whatever the design of the interview checklist there is invariably insufficient space to record all data, so some form of understandable shorthand should be used. To be productive and time-efficient, the data on the form should always reflect the closeness or otherwise to the benchmark of the person specification. This functionally restricts the notes to information that is directly relevant to the applicant's suitability.

It is helpful to standardize the notemaking. The interviewer should try always to comment on a particular aspect of the various candidates in the same way and on the same area of the checklist.

## Specialist Help

***Question: How important is testing to the skilled interviewer?***

Psychometric testing is an invaluable tool in the process of selection. The tests help in identifying and assessing candidates' intellectual and educational skills, aptitudes and manual dexterity, intelligence, colour blindness, and personality characteristics. Tests are available for a very wide range of candidates, from early school leavers with no academic qualifications, through to senior management levels. Tests are designed for graduate entry candidates; for people with varied technical competence; for handicapped people with physical, motor or auditory disability.

Testing should not be a substitute for the selection interview. The value lies in providing interviewers with reliable in-depth information on different human aspects in a relatively short time.

Some examples of tests are as follows:

- *Graduate and managerial assessment.* Manager-level candidates are assessed to see how well they can absorb information given in semi-technical reports and then take appropriate action.
- *Appraisal of verbal and numerical awareness for clerical, secretarial, administrative and supervisory staff.* Candidates are assessed on how accurately and how quickly printed information can be checked and coded.
- *Appraisal of non-verbal reasoning skills.* Tests at supervisory and junior management levels identify ability to reason that is least affected by background, previous education and culture.

- *Appraisal of intellectual reasoning skills.* Tests for junior and middle managers identify how well candidates are able to tackle different reasoning tasks.
- *Assessment of basic numeracy and literacy skills.* These tests are for unskilled candidates and for candidates of different ethnic groups.
- *Appraisal of mechanical reasoning.* Different tests for apprentices and technical trainees identify levels of technical understanding and the ability to diagnose faults independent of prior technical knowledge.
- *Appraisal of technological potential.* Tests specifically designed to identify candidates with the potential to work with computers.
- *Assessment of people with disabilities.* These tests are designed for persons with hearing, visual and motor disabilities.
- *Assessment of personality.* This testing provides a personality profile of candidates, giving discrete behavioural characteristics.

A short list of suppliers of tests is given at the end of this chapter. The examples given above are a small proportion of the available tests; where appropriate new selection or appraisal tests can be designed, to help recruitment, say, for a new demanding management role. It is also possible to formalize and validate in-house testing procedures developed by organizations for their own use. To be effective, all psychometric tests must be properly applied and correctly interpreted. For those without a background of psychology, help in understanding and operating psychometric testing procedures is available from the test material suppliers, who mount training and familiarization courses for the administration of their tests. Literature and general information is available from The British Psychological Society, 48 Princes Road East, Leicester LE1 7DR (Tel. 0533-549 568).

## No-escape Homework

***Question: What interview preparations are critical to success?***

Successful interviewing is easy, as long as the homework is done. Success is measured by the selection of the candidate that is best for the job — it is not measured by interviews that:

- Finish quickly.
- Are interesting.
- Identify common interests.
- Involve sexually attractive candidates.

- Identify third parties of common acquaintance.
- Demonstrate proper respect for the interviewer.
- Promise private benefit for the interviewer.

Many interviewers without experience are apprehensive, when faced with the task of interviewing and recruitment; not all admit to such fears. In the very first interview, these worries are quickly allayed because candidates will be seen to provide no threat. As a general rule, rarely proved wrong, candidates do everything in their power to impress the interviewer with courtesy, respect and whatever charm can be mustered. Remember that candidates themselves will always be nervous, though some may manage to disguise their fears successfully.

Because candidates are polite, smile and answer questions, the interviewer must not assume that the interview is necessarily going well. The objective of an interview is to uncover and identify all the information about a candidate's background, work experience, skills, motivation, aspirations and suitability that allows a 'correct' decision. Interviews conducted without prior preparation and without a structure are unlikely to be totally effective. But the interviewer does not know this at the time: events arising from poor selection decisions do not appear until much later. Poor selection decisions can mean:

- Candidates who are not capable of meeting the job requirements intellectually or physically or with enough skill.
- Candidates who cannot work with colleagues.
- Candidates who resent authority.
- Candidates who are too shy or lack minimal social graces.
- Candidates who are dishonest or untruthful.
- Candidates lacking motivation.
- Candidates with strong racial prejudice.
- Aggressively sexist candidates.

It is useful to keep an abbreviated checklist of these items, to look at before the candidate is dismissed. If the interviewer is unsure of a judgement on any of these points, further questions can be asked.

In advance of the interview, the interviewer should:

1. Arrange or delegate responsibility for the administration of the following items:

    - An interview room and suitable furniture.
    - Privacy.

- Diversion of telephone calls.
- Car parking arrangements.
- A candidate rota and timetable allowing adequate time for each interview.
- The reception of candidates, with provision of an adequate waiting area.
- Company literature or documentation for distribution to candidates.
- A float for payment of travel expenses.
- Ensure that all necessary documentation — e.g. Employee's Handbook, sales literature, etc. — is available.

2. Read the interviewee's application form or CV, correspondence, and the job description and specification — and check the Interview Assessment Form, and complete it if unfinished.

These items are of paramount importance. It is not sufficient to wait and ask the candidate to supply the information during the interview. Are there any gaps or 'fudging' in the CV? For example: 'Read 3 yr. B.Sc. honours degree course in chemistry.' Did the candidate actually graduate? If not, what are the reasons why the course was not completed? Careful wording is frequently used by candidates to suggest an enhanced interpretation of actual events. On occasion there are gaps in a candidate's education or work experience. The sequence given in the CV is 'rounded off' to present the candidate history as one of positive development. Are there any gaps? What is the reason for these gaps?

3. Having studied the Interview Assessment form prepare:

   (a) A list of the areas that must be probed to explain the difference, if any, between the candidate specification and the person specification. The candidate can be asked how he or she reconciles any difference.
   (b) A few open questions that help to qualify and understand the strengths and weaknesses of the candidate. Many open questions will be asked in the course of the interview but a prompt list, to hand, is often found to be useful.
   (c) A personal agenda for the interview session. Any temptation to dispense with the agenda as unnecessary must be strongly resisted.

Although all interviewers will be 100 per cent sure that they are blameless, a sin committed by many is wandering from the path. An agenda contributes to discipline, particularly when timings are added for each stage. An agenda that works is:

- Preliminaries to relax the candidate.
- The interviewer's description of the company.
- Administration of selection tests if not previously undertaken.
- Discussion and confirmation of candidate's CV.
- Detailed discussion of the job vacancy in relation to the candidate's potential contribution.
- Negotiation, if appropriate, of the terms of the appointment.
- Free questions from the candidate.
- A statement of when the candidate is going to hear the result — whether appointment, second interview or rejection.
- Payment of candidate's travel claim.

The Interview Assessment form is structured on five major person points. Some interviewers increase this to seven, adding the categories of 'First impressions' and 'Motivation'. Novice interviewers should experiment, following up after the employment of the successful candidate to validate which method of assessment proved most effective and the most comfortable to use.

If the interview is to be by a panel — i.e. with more than one interviewer present — decide in advance who is to ask questions on which aspects. For example, financial, marketing or technical skills may be specifically probed by a colleague other than the interviewer. When it is cost-effective to use more than one interviewer at the same interview session, the likelihood of making the best decisions is increased. Sometimes, when there are many candidates, interviews are conducted in parallel by different interviewers of the panel, who interview each candidate in turn according to a pre-planned schedule. The results are then compared to enable decisions to be made.

With group interviews, candidates are brought together and collectively given an exercise problem to resolve. Their performance is observed by a panel of assessors. The Civil Service, the Armed Forces and some companies make much use of this type of interview to identify candidates with leadership, problem-solving and management strengths. Group interviews are a useful procedure in the selection process for internal promotion. There are a number of specialist training companies that can assist in setting up tailor-made group interviews. Their names are in the *National Training And Consultancy Index* published by Graduate Group Ltd, 1st Floor, 25 Poland Street, London W1V 3DB (Tel. 071-287 2172).

## A Winning Formula

***Question: How do good interviewers conduct their interviews?***

The opening minutes of an interview are particularly important. How well a candidate controls initial nervousness is a useful indicator of temperament. Body language is giving out messages all the time, of which the candidate may not even be aware. Interviewers should take on board the first impression: in many cases this will be enhanced as candidates' confidence grows, their apprehension is controlled and the positive strengths and qualities emerge.

An experienced interviewer influences the process of relaxation positively. Informal icebreaker questions can be asked: 'Did you find us easily?', 'How do you like this glorious weather?' Simple non-taxing questions let the candidate gain confidence from hearing the sound of his or her own voice. The opening moments of the interview are intended to be relaxing. Within this period the interviewer should explain the procedures for the interview. If there is more than one interviewer, the colleagues are introduced by name or function. It is not necessary that they speak at this stage.

Unless deliberately employed in order to monitor the reaction, leading questions likely to influence the response should be avoided. For example 'I take it you approve of government legislation curbing the powers of trade unions?' will probably invite a 'Yes' answer.

Sometimes an inspection of the workplace or site is appropriate. The interviewer should decide whether the visit is to take place before the interview so that a candidate's reactions can be discussed, or at a later time. One option is to restrict inspection visits to those candidates likely to be employed, or at least marked to return for a second interview.

It is helpful to take brief notes, particularly when there are many candidates to be interviewed. The Interview Assessment form is useful when making the selection assessment, but some find that the available space for making notes during the interview is too small. A separate A4 pad can be used, with the pre-planned probing open questions written at the top. After each interview the notes are condensed and written up on the Interview Assessment form. Candidates should always be told that notes are necessary in the context of the selection process. Although the interviewer sets the interview rules, reference to note-taking removes any unintentional perceived threat. For the same reason it is best not to write adverse reactions down immediately, as this will cause the candidate to become anxious. At all times it should be ensured that the candidate cannot read the interviewer's notes.

When candidates appear for interview, some are skilful enough to make sure the interviewer is made aware of all of their strengths. Others fail to find the opportunity to describe all their plusses, and the interviewer may not have probed adequately. One question to help candidates give the information they consider important is: 'Are there any questions that you expected to be asked in this interview, for which you are keen to give your answers, but which haven't yet been asked?' Another useful question to encourage candidates to reveal their self-image is: 'How do you rate your performance in this interview up till now?' The initial response is usually modest, but further direct questions on the reasons for modesty will highlight the candidates' perception of their skills.

Good interviewers are aware of, and compensate for, a bias known as the 'halo effect'. This is the tendency to over-rate candidates who went to the same school or university, served in the same regiment, or played the same sport as the interviewer. Similarly it under-rates candidates with no such background. The halo effect is ignored by experienced interviewers but the novice interviewer preparing for the first interview assignment should beware of it.

## Wrapping Up

***Question: What are the salient points of the offer of employment?***

Offers of employment should always be confirmed in writing. If the offer is conditional upon the receipt of satisfactory references, passing a medical examination or completing a probationary period, this should be mentioned in the letter. Under the Employment Protection (Consolidation) Act 1978, as amended by the Employment Act 1982, within 13 weeks of starting work the employee is to be provided with a written statement of terms and conditions.

It is common practice to combine the information contained within the statement with the offer of employment itself. In this way the successful candidate has from the start all the necessary information on terms and conditions of employment and eliminates the need for an additional statement.

All offers of employment should be accepted by the candidate, in writing, prior to the commencement of employment. An example of an 'offer letter' is shown in Figure 3.4.

Dear Mr ...

With reference to your recent interview I am pleased to confirm the position of Shop-Floor Operative to commence on 1st July, 1995, based at our main road site. Your Job Description is attached. You should report at...(time) to ...(name of Shift Manager/Supervisor)... on Monday, 1st July. Your previous employment does not count as part of your continuous employment.

Your basic wage is £180.00 per week, paid one week in arrears, each Friday, into a bank account of your choosing. Any overtime worked Monday to Saturday will be paid at time and one half. Sunday working is paid at double time.

You are working a two-shift system – 6.00 am to 2.00 pm and 2.00 pm to 10.00 pm which carries a premium payment of 20 per cent on the basic wage.

You are entitled to payment for eight statutory holidays. Annual holiday entitlement is 25 days for 12 months' service. Less than 12 months' service is calculated at 2 days per completed calendar month.

After completing 12 months' service you are entitled to Company Sick Pay. This consists of basic wage less State Benefits up to a maximum of 12 weeks in any 12-month period.

After three months' service you are eligible to join the Company Pension Scheme, details of which will be provided on joining the Company.

Your notice entitlement by the Company is one week's notice, rising to 12 weeks' notice, for each year of completed service. You are required to give the Company one week's notice.

The disciplinary rules which apply to you are contained in the Company Disciplinary Procedure. A copy is attached.

Should you have a grievance about your employment you should in the first instance discuss it with your Shift Manager. If you cannot resolve your grievance you may request a meeting with your Factory Manager.

At your Induction you will receive copies of all relevant procedures and agreements which affect your employment.

This offer of employment is subject to your passing a Company medical test and the Company receiving satisfactory references.

Please confirm your acceptance of this offer in writing. We look forward to your joining the Company.

Yours sincerely

J.B.Heathcoate
PERSONNEL MANAGER

*Figure 3.4. A sample offer letter.*

## Summary

*Question:* What routine tasks precede the selection interview?
*Answer:* Before the selection interview applicants are screened for allocation into 'interview', 'immediate rejection' and 'borderline' groups. Standard letters are sent to the first two groups. An Interview Assessment form is prepared as an essential working document for the interviewer.

*Question:* How important is testing to the skilled interviewer?
*Answer:* Psychometric tests, when properly administered and correctly interpreted, are very helpful as an adjunct to, but not a substitute for, professional interviewing skills. The function of tests is to identify and assess intellectual, technical and educational skills, aptitudes, manual dexterity, colour blindness, intelligence, and personality characteristics.

*Question:* What interview preparations are critical to success?
*Answer:* There are four aspects of preparation: (1) attend to a number of administrative details relating to the interview room venue and reception of candidates; (2) read the candidate's documents before the interview; (3) plan the structure of the interview, prepare a number of major probing open questions, and write down an interview agenda; (4) when interviewing as a panel, arrange beforehand the tasks for each interviewer.

*Question:* How do good interviewers conduct their interviews?
*Answer:* Good interviewers ensure at the outset that candidates are relaxed. They follow their own interview agenda, probing to secure an unbiased picture of candidates' history, personal skills and potential for the position desired. Notes are taken. Good interviewers take particular care to see that unattractive personality traits or poor social skills not instantly apparent are not present to detract from job performance if the candidate is employed.

*Question:* What are the salient points of the offer of employment?
*Answer:* Offers of employment are confirmed in writing and must be accepted in writing before employment begins. Within 13 weeks of commencement, employees must be provided with a written statement of terms and conditions. This statement may be incorporated in the offer of employment.

## Suppliers of Psychometric Tests

Mercuri Urval — 29 Grovehill Road, Harrow HA1 1YZ (Tel. 081-863 8466).
The Psychological Corporation — Foots Cray, High Street, Sidcup DA14 5HP (Tel. 081-300 1149).
Saville & Holdsworth — The Old Post House, 21 High Street, Esher KT10 9QA (Tel. 0372-68634).
The Test Agency — Cournswood House, North Dean, High Wycombe HP14 4NW (Tel. 0494-563384).
Walpole Occupational Psychologists — 61-63 St John Street, London EC1M 4AN (Tel. 071-253 2340).

# Part 2

# CREATING ADDED-VALUE EMPLOYEES

# 4

# TRAINING

Please answer the following questions before reading this chapter. The questions are worked through in the text. The answers are collected together in a summary at the end of the chapter.

## Questions

- In an organization what added-value benefits are derived from the training function?
- How are training needs assessed at organizational level?
- How are individual training needs assessed?
- What are the major training strategies?
- What is NVQ – how does it help?

## You Get What You Pay For

***Question: In an organization what added-value benefits are derived from the training function?***

In terms of training, Great Britain is very near the bottom of the class. In the countries of major competitors such as America, Japan,

Germany and France many more top managers have technical and degree qualifications and many more school leavers have higher qualifications than in the United Kingdom. The number of 'on the job' training days, in percentage terms, is lowest in Britain too. The problem will not just go away: to make matters worse, it is being compounded. In the last two decades United Kingdom industry, in the pattern of tradition, has been used to planning for the arrival of the new workforce intake with their new learned skills. Instead, in the 1990s we are faced with a falling population of school leavers — and there are ongoing major changes in technology, making existing workforce skills outmoded.

A major tool to counter sluggish industry is training. Training within an organization brings benefits on many fronts. At the simplest level it provides an individual with skills. The result of that training invests the individual with an increased value in the labour market, with a better self-image, and brings enhanced opportunity for continuing employment.

Training is complex, with objectives ranging through management, professional and technical development. Success from training is a function of many factors:

- How well training needs are identified.
- How effectively and how frequently training is delivered.
- The success of the recruitment policy in providing staff of an appropriate calibre.
- The training budget.
- The availability of training venues and resources.
- The support of senior management.
- The support of the workforce.
- The support of the unions.

When the training is successful benefits to the organization will include:

*Increased production.* When the workforce all have learned the skills necessary to their job function, the work rate may be quicker. It is likely too that fewer mistakes will be made. But training does not only refer to specific work skills. Communication skills and supervisory and management function are enhanced by training, and make their own contributions to increased production.

*Fewer industrial accidents.* Strict adherence to safety codes and safe working practice, achieved through training, brings a reduction in accidents or their total avoidance.

*Heightened job satisfaction.* Doing a job well brings pride and self-respect — more so when the skill is newly learned.

*Generally raised morale.* Teams that are trained to work efficiently and work well create a buzz. Everyone is involved. The beginning of each new workday is no longer a chore.

*Reduced labour turnover.* Generally, new staff represent the highest number of leavers. Good training and concern by the company about the rate of learning in the induction period help to reduce the number of staff leaving through failure to achieve.

*Staff retention.* Changes in technology and changes in market fashion create situations where many members of staff are no longer able to make an adequate contribution. Retraining helps to reduce the pressures on staff and their motivation to seek less stressful alternative employment.

*Positive public image.* Good public relations occasionally occur spontaneously, but a company needs a favourable public image all the time. A structured PR programme with dedicated training of company personnel can manipulate the perception of the public in a positive way. A sound public image facilitates the recruitment of new staff as well as a demand for the company's products or services.

*Awareness of the customer as No. 1.* Traditionally workers on the shop floor are remote from customer service. An orientation of all in the company to customer needs, as reflected by a high quality of product and supporting service, stems from senior management. The 'customer' philosophy is achieved through upgraded job specifications and tailored training for both management and the workforce.

The list continues. Other results of effective staff training are, for the individual, increased job security, a better self-image and increased opportunities for promotion. For the organization the projected outcome of structured straining programmes is progress in the market place, with increasing staff loyalty and pride.

A good illustration of the benefits of sound training is seen with Cheswood Produce Ltd, winners of a national training award. The company are mushroom growers. Their training mission statement proclaims that every employee is to have the necessary skills to perform his or her job to the best of his or her ability.

The results they achieved from their training programme are:

- Labour turnover reduced by 18 per cent over a three-year period, making a significant saving in recruitment and training costs.
- Health and safety improved with a reduction in days lost due to accidents: the numbers reduced from 300 to 158 over a period of three years.
- Through training the supervisor's role was enhanced. This allowed the company to reduce the management establishment by 10 posts.
- Quality standards were raised through improved training. A direct result attributed to this progress was an additional £200,000 in revenue.
- Operatives preparing compost for growing increased their knowledge and awareness of the process. A direct result was a cost reduction of 6 per cent in one year.
- Improved production and quality was achieved, with subsequent reduction in training time, by detailed attention to the procedures for picking and packing.
- Customer/supplier relationships were improved through specific training in customer care for delivery drivers.

Offsetting the benefits of all training, good and bad, is cost. In the larger companies, with permanent training establishments, there are fixed costs — rent, the salaries of permanent training staff, and audio-visual and other training resources. There are the variable costs applicable to companies large and small, of ad hoc training resources and consultant trainer fees. In addition there are peripheral costs that may have some significance: these can be the costs of lost production through worker or staff absence in training sessions, and the wages costs of induction or apprenticeship training.

## A Positive Approach

### *Question: How are training needs assessed at organizational level?*

In an ideal world a company will have a foolproof human resource plan. This coordinates training, retraining, recruitment and career development so that competent experienced trained staff are always available as needed. A starting point to achieve this desirable position is a company-wide training needs analysis. In practical terms the training audit embraces four categories of training need:

1. *On-the-job training*. Discussions with the line manager will identify appropriate training for new recruits. From the job description for

any particular job, a list can be prepared of the skills, knowledge and attitudes that a person doing the job should possess. So in terms of the training that is required it is necessary to know the skills, knowledge and attitudes of the person who is to be trained to carry out the work. Even when training precedents are established, it is helpful to ask questions on the approach to be adopted. Is the present system acceptable? How can the rate of learning and degree of confidence of trainees be enhanced?

2. *Training to improve performance.* How can workers with experience — some set in their ways, some indifferent, others simply frustrated — be helped to increase output? Indicators from appraisal records, from counselling interviews, from discussions with the line manager — and particularly with the employee — contribute to the assessment of training needs.

3. *Development training.* Staff with the potential to undertake greater responsibility can be helped by training. The line manager and higher management should define through appraisal the skills, knowledge and attitudes for the job to which promotion is possible. Development training also has immediate relevance when fresh responsibilities are added to an existing job.

4. *Training because of change.* An example here is when a road haulage company makes a decision to buy a new type of vehicle, with sophisticated handling systems, greater capacity and different operating and maintenance systems. The success of the operation depends on new skills being learned by drivers, by maintenance engineers, by handling staff, by warehousemen, and new practices being adopted by the customers being served. The implications for training have to be identified at the outset.

Within information technology there are continuing training needs to meet change. Learning keyboard skills, using new computer software and new telephone switchboards are all ongoing requirements.

A useful way to analyse training needs is by a matrix format as illustrated in Figure 4.1

It is obviously advantageous if the organization has an established training division. An organizational training needs analysis can then be conducted as a straightforward exercise making use of existing training personnel. If the company is starting from scratch with a new training officer, some obstacles may be encountered from employees or from line managers who believe their authority may be threatened.

The extent of such problems, if they exist, may depend on whether the new training officer is an existing manager seconded to the training role or a person newly recruited. In a difficult situation every effort has to be made to identify and allay any fears encountered.

As organizations begin to grow, the impetus to taking training seriously is often triggered by a hiccup in expansion or profits growth. For example, product delivery costs may be too high through clumsy handling procedures, or potential customers are alienated by indifferent or sloppy staff contact. A training officer is appointed specifically to resolve the immediate problem. When the problem has been addressed, it is then logical to follow up and evaluate training needs for the entire organization, to pre-empt the next obstacles to company growth.

| | Skill | Knowledge | Attitude |
|---|---|---|---|
| On-the-job Training | | | |
| Improving Performance | | | |
| Development | | | |
| Training for Change | | | |

*Figure 4.1. Training needs analysis matrix.*

There are implications, also to be addressed, in the Health & Safety at Work Act 1974, Part 1, Section 2. There is legislation that safety training must be an integral part of a company's training schemes. Particular reference is made to induction programmes, operator training and the training programmes for managers and supervisors. To cover this aspect, an awareness is necessary of the total organizational training needs.

Whether the audit is undertaken informally in the smaller company, or with the authority of a large established training department, it takes place in four stages (see Figure 4.2).

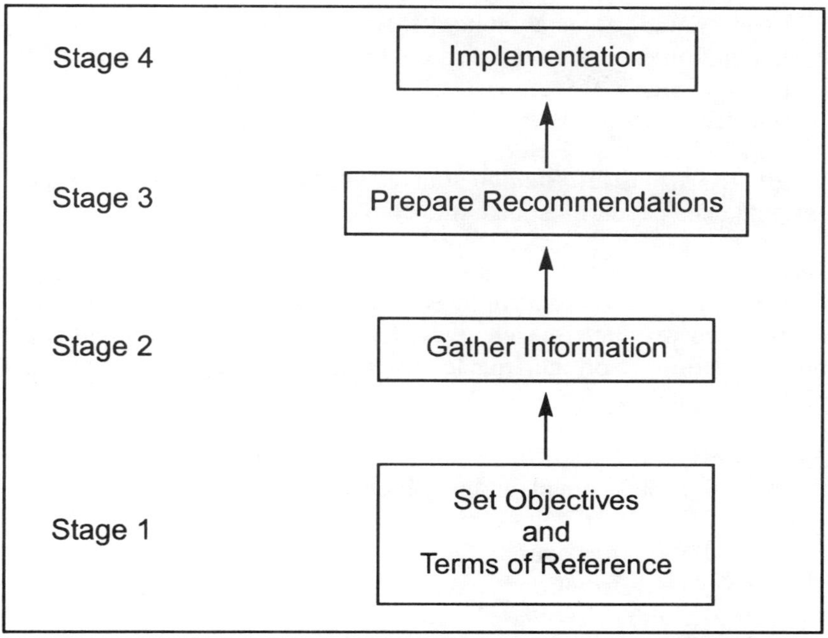


*Figure 4.2. Stages of the organizational training needs audit.*

### *Stage 1. Set audit objectives and terms of reference*

The brief will clearly set out the scope of the audit, what must be achieved, the timescale, methods of information gathering and the degree of confidentiality. It should be written formally. In practical terms the author of the report is investigating the operational efficiency of the organization, the effectiveness of present training, and what training is needed for future progress.

### *Stage 2. Gather information*

The research exercise is fairly complex — the information has to be gleaned, extricated, observed, deduced, calculated, analysed and sometimes wheedled. Although the data is there within the company's activities and records — and externally in economic and market trends — it is not always neatly packaged and labelled, ready for evaluation. The training officer has a range of methods to secure information:

- Interviews.
- Sifting though departmental records of personnel statistics of absenteeism, accidents, appraisal, industrial relations disputes.
- Reading training committee reports.
- Sifting through minutes of management policy meetings.

- Reading trade association market reports.
- Evaluating previous organizational training audits.
- Discussions with senior management in production, sales and finance.

There are various information sources which the author of an organizational needs audit must take into consideration:

*Senior management.* It is necessary to know divisional objectives, and the strategic plans to achieve those objectives. Information is required on planned product line changes, technological changes and their projected impact on staffing levels, marketing policy changes and planned capital expenditure.

*Employee statistics and information.* This is normally available from the personnel department, and will include:

(a) Labour turnover.
(b) Age distribution.
(c) Length of service.
(d) Remuneration policies.
(e) Job descriptions.
(f) Job specifications.
(g) Promotion policies.

These statistics are of particular importance to the audit. There are implications of induction and job training, for example, when there is a high turnover of new staff. The length of service leavers table may give a pointer to current training inadequacy if many staff are leaving after only a short time with the company. Another reason for staff leaving could be poor selection at interview. In this case training is indicated for those conducting the interviews.

*Specialist service departments.* Information from the accounting, quality control, R & D, organization and method departments is all of value to the training officer. A breakdown of training expenditure and costs provides indicators of successful or ineffectual training activities. Work study conclusions give pointers to future training needs. Human resource implications lie in R & D findings in relation to new technology and retraining needs.

*Line management.* The managers and supervisors in daily contact with existing training activities are well placed to comment on training successes and unsatisfied training needs.

*The external market place.* The consumers of the products and services of the organization cannot be ignored. When demand increases, recruitment and training follow. In boom time, adequate skilled staff cannot be attracted and intensive in-house training is a serious option. When the market is depressed and demand low, training will shrink. Information should be gathered from clients, and from the wide range of economic, political and industrial press and publications.

### *Stage 3. Prepare recommendations*

When all the data is gathered it must be evaluated. Recommendations should be formulated and set out in report format. This task is not easy: invariably departmental managers press for training budget priority with persuasive arguments; overall, there will be budgetary constraints. So both existing and new training projects need to be costed. Questions should be asked and answered: What is available in-house, over what time span? What external training agencies can be bought in? Realistically, how effectively can the training department with its existing complement of staff achieve training objectives? Is there a case for recruiting additional training staff?

In preparing his plan the training officer knows that organizational training objectives and departmental training objectives are all subordinate to meeting the aims and objectives of the organization as a whole. If senior management agree the plan and grant the training spend, will the organization go forward in a planned advance?

In evaluation of the data and preparation of training recommendations, full consideration has to be given to every influencing factor:

- What industry or government grants are available?
- How disruptive is training to production and administration?
- What are the costs in order of training priorities?
- What are the projected benefits?
- What happens if training is withheld?
- What is the staff perception of the value of training?
- What is management's perception of training?
- What level of criticism can be published on training failures within the company?
- What proportion of a training budget is best allocated to hardware (audio-visual equipment, books, etc.) and what to fees?
- Is self-financing training feasible, with each department meeting its own training costs?

### *Stage 4. Implementation*

The final stage generally only comes after the training officer has argued, justified and fought for his report and proposals. In difficult trading times particularly there will be competing demands for the budget allocation.

It is helpful if the report can define criteria for evaluating the effectiveness of training. In some cases evaluation is easy — the number of imperfect custard pies in a production line can be counted before and after training. In the medium term, statistical analysis of labour turnover, absenteeism, lateness, accidents, or customer complaints can be linked to the effectiveness of management and supervisor training.

Some results of training are more difficult to evaluate — for example, its effects on management initiative or the industrial relations climate. The farther one moves from testing the effect of training on an individual, who can be tested, observed and asked for his or her own subjective opinion of performance, the more difficult it becomes to assess training influence accurately. The successful organizational training needs report addresses the spectrum of training evaluation in detail.

## Grass Roots

### *Question: How are individual training needs assessed?*

In organizational training, individual training needs are the nuts to which training bolts are applied. To design appropriate training it is necessary to analyse a job to know what skills and what knowledge are required for that job at any specific time. The value of job analysis is greatest at the lower levels of an organization because supervisory or management decision-making play little or no part there. Indeed, at the higher levels job analysis is best described in terms of the objectives to be met.

Some jobs have few basic component tasks; others have many. Some require frequent change; others necessitate a degree of formal education. As a starting point jobs can be categorized into:

(a) Manual jobs.
(b) Interpersonal jobs.
(c) Decision-making jobs.

They are then broken down into 'tasks', 'sub-tasks' and 'elements'. Figure 4.3 illustrates such components for the interpersonal job of

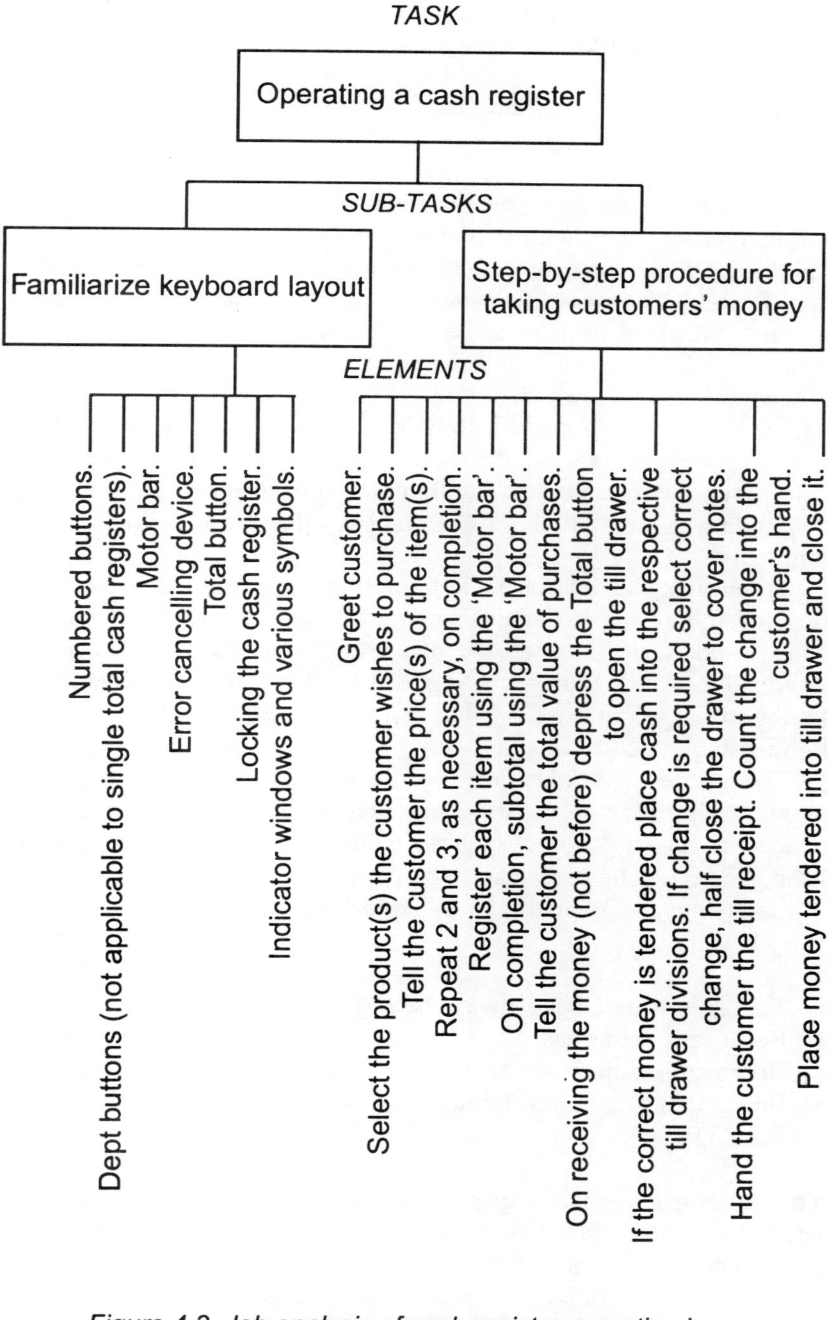


*Figure 4.3. Job analysis of cash register operation in a supermarket checkout.*

operating a cash register in a supermarket checkout. Here two major sub-tasks are identified:

1. Learning the layout of the cash-register keys.
2. Step-by-step procedures for taking customers' money.

Each task is then broken down in to its key elements. The analysis is subjective, and the depth of the analysis is at the discretion of the training officer. For example, Element 9 of the Step-by-step procedure for taking customers' money is defined as 'If the correct money is tendered place cash into the respective till drawer divisions. If change....' The element might be extended to incorporate a standard procedure in respect of handling the money in descending order of value. Highest denomination monies are always stored or tendered first. In the example used, the training department of the supermarket considered that learning the additional step of dealing with money in descending denomination gave no added value to the task, so it was omitted.

When mistakes that occur in the job prove costly to the organization the training needs analysis should incorporate a faults analysis. This comprises a detailed list of all the faults that can occur, the implications of the fault occurring, and steps to be taken to ensure that faults do not occur. A flow diagram is particularly helpful in highlighting fault occurrence.

The process of job analysis to find the tasks, sub-tasks and elements is prone to creating hostility if the aims of the training officer are not explained. When the confidence of the job operator has been gained it is helpful to ask why particular actions are incorporated in the task cycle. Elements of a sub-task may be executed in certain ways because:

- That is how they have always been done.
- Because it seems easy.
- Because the supervisor says so.
- Because of physical difficulty with alternative action.
- For no known reason.

The general response may provide clues to the nature of training needed, or to the fact that training is not needed at all. Sometimes poor performance is not due to impoverished skill but to lack of adequate administrative or organizational support. An example is the repeated failure of a mail order company to type addresses and despatch the post in time to catch the evening collection. Preliminary analysis suggested that the cause was inadequate typing skills — a fault that could be rectified by training. Analysis of the sequence of events in fact disclosed that the real problem, frequently repeated, was one of securing appropriate address labels in sufficient time. When this difficulty was addressed, the post was despatched without delays.

In every analysis the opinions of the line manager should be sought, initially, as to what training is needed. The training officer is wise to be circumspect: generally such opinions will be valuable, but there are circumstances when the supervisor or manager has insufficient experience to be wholly accurate.

Job analysis to identify training needs may go into greater depth than an analysis to provide the job description and job specification essential to recruitment. But each document has its value. Analysis for identifying training needs establishes the 'what' and the 'how' of the job. It is also important to know why the job is done — perhaps there are better ways of meeting the job objectives.

## The Best Way

***Question: What are the major training strategies?***

The implications of training and retraining for human resource planning are considerable. Faced with an increasing shortage of skilled manpower, the training department has to create its own supply of well-trained staff. This it does, through courses that may range from half a day to three months.

### *Induction training*

Any person starting a new job — whether for the first time or by transferring from another job — requires some form of induction training. It helps a new employee become familiar with the job, the people on the job, the workplace surroundings, the organization itself and the industry. This initial training is very important. It is a key to effective employee performance and employee retention, yet too many organizations ignore induction training or have poor induction procedures.

Generally, induction training is presented informally so as to reduce tensions for the new employee, but it should be structured systematically to ensure that the employee is exposed to all the relevant aspects of the organization. Those planning the induction programme may include the personnel officer, training officer, supervisor or line manager, wages supervisor, safety officer and trade union representative.

The reception and welcome on the first day of the induction

Name of new employee........................................................
Start date .................. Department.......................................

Induction personnel ........................
........................
........................

Signature ________

1. RECEPTION
- Welcome ________
- Personal documentation ________
- Contract of employment ________
- Staff handbook ________
- Introduction to:
  - Works Manager ________
  - Departmental Head ________
  - Supervisor ________
  - Training Officer ________
- First aid arrangements ________
- Fire drill ________

2. ORIENTATION
- Tour of premises ________
- Entrances and exits ________
- Canteen facilities ________
- Cloakroom facilities ________
- Telephone facilities ________
- Car/bicycle park ________
- Notice boards ________

3. CONDITIONS OF WORK
- Company rules ________
- Employment contract explained ________
- Clocking in ________
- Pay slip explained ________
- Eligibility for overtime payment ________
- Holidays ________
- Sickness procedure ________
- Sick pay ________
- Discipline procedure ________
- Grievance procedure ________
- Safety hazards ________

| | |
|---|---|
| 4. WORK DEPARTMENT | |
| Inductee's job | ______ |
| Colleagues | ______ |
| Supervision | ______ |
| Job target | ______ |
| Job standard | ______ |
| Department function in relation to company | ______ |
| 5. TRAINING | |
| Company training scheme | ______ |
| External training facilities | ______ |
| Opportunities for qualifications | ______ |
| Opportunities for promotion | ______ |
| 6. THE ORGANIZATION | |
| Company structure | ______ |
| Directors and management | ______ |
| Products, services and markets | ______ |
| 7. EMPLOYEE BENEFITS | |
| Medical services | ______ |
| Purchase of company products | ______ |
| Sports/social facilities | ______ |
| Transport arrangements | ______ |
| Protective clothing | ______ |
| Pension scheme | |
| 8. TRADE UNIONS | |
| Trade union recognition | ______ |
| Union representatives | ______ |
| Trade union procedures | ______ |

*Figure 4.4. Induction training checklist.*

process is important, but induction is often spread over several days or weeks. Most young employees have no idea of how their job relates to other jobs in the company, or how it will develop. But there are limits to the amount of information that can be absorbed in a short time. There are also constraints in arranging time off from shift work, or interrupting the impetus of new job enthusiasm. The induction process is designed to give an orientation, to instil confidence, and to provide direction and appropriate training for the job of work being started.

To ensure that the induction programme successfully meets its objectives, a detailed checklist should be prepared. The parties concerned should be named and told to initial or tick off the induction aspects for which they are responsible. Figure 4.4 illustrates a model checklist, which may be adapted to reflect specific organization needs. In a small company the induction period is invariably shorter than in a large or headquarters organization.

### *On-the-job training*

Traditionally called 'sitting next to Nellie', learning through on-the-job training is achieved by working in a real work environment with an experienced person.

The principle of on-the-job training is sound. For example, a novice salesman is taken out by an experienced salesman to learn how to find customers and sell to them. Many of the practical skills of selling — talking to customers, getting past protective secretaries, taking orders, selling to reluctant buyers, increasing order sizes — are only mastered through real life experience. On-the-job training has very wide application where the specification of the job is not highly technical.

On a production line, disadvantages of this method may be a level of wasted materials and production may be slowed down or disrupted. On the positive side there is very good learning transfer, training costs are insignificant, and the trainee is learning in the work environment. For practical reasons, management should first consider giving training instruction to the supervisors or senior workers entrusted with the 'Nellie' role. For example, in instruction for driving a car, a trained instructor is invariably more effective than a person qualified only by practical driving experience.

### *Off-the-job training*

In order not to disrupt the production flow, a simulated shop floor is set up away from the main production line. Trainees are given the opportunity to become familiar with operating procedures and skills, under instruction, but their initial efforts do not spoil or disrupt. Off-the-job training differs from on-the-job training in that it is usually a much longer process. The training is delivered in the organization's own training premises, as well as away at a college or technical institute.

## *In-house training*

In-house training describes training that is specifically tailored to meet the needs of the organization. Despite the name, in-house training is not delivered only at the organization's own premises: courses are also run at universities, colleges, management centres or hotels. Nor is such training provided only by personnel of the organization's own training department. Complementary training skills are found from outside training agencies as well from a large body of independent training organizations that advertise in the press. A useful source of reference is the *National Training Directory* published by Macmillan Publishers Ltd, Houndsmill, Basingstoke, Hants RG21 2XS (Tel. 0256-29242).

In-house training generally covers management and supervisory training, graduate induction, and interpersonal skills. Other courses meet specific needs such as developments in industrial relations or changes in technology or accountancy practice.

Good in-house training addresses the problems and opportunities faced by the organization. Outside training providers tend to have a portfolio of courses. Good training providers can adapt such courses to meet an organization's specific needs. To achieve this match it is important that specific training objectives are set by the training department that must be met by the outside training agency. It is also helpful for the trainer concerned to spend time at the organization, in advance of the course, talking to management and some of the intended trainees. For in-house sales training, the trainer should spend at least a day accompanying a representative working in the field.

Where budgetary constraints are not the prime consideration, sophisticated in-house courses will include specially prepared video-film to be used as a training resource. Such films can create real life situations faced by the company, reinforced by role play and other training exercises. Realism is enhanced by inviting managers from the organization to role-play themselves or other managers as the film is made.

## *External training*

Training required by an organization that is not available in-house can be bought in from outside suppliers, in just the same way that raw materials or other services are purchased. There are three types of external course:

1. *Short courses*. A length of one to three days is the most common but some courses designed for senior management extend from one to three weeks. As unit costs (namely, day rate charges) for each partici-

pant are high, care is appropriate in assessing the effectiveness of the training suppliers. The objectives should be carefully studied to see that they match those of the organization, and efforts should be made to evaluate the effectiveness of the trainers employed — there is often an element of trial and error.

There are persuasive arguments in favour of sending employees out to external courses, even where the learning transfer proves not to be of the highest order. Participation in a group with delegates from other industries, different backgrounds, different working environments and diverse experience, generates valuable cross-fertilization of ideas and perceptions. Moreover, if the course is residential there can be a positive social element. An important message to the participant, even if unstated, is that the organization cares about its employees.

A valuable facet of external training is that single participants may be sent away on a course. But when the numbers requiring training in any specific discipline reach to, say, six or more, the cost may equal to that required for delivery of an in-house course. The training manager should therefore decide on the option that is most appropriate.

2. *Study courses leading to qualifications.* The courses may extend to six or twelve months, or longer. Modular courses are coming increasingly popular. With many that lead to degree qualifications the part-time study culminates in one or two weeks' absence from work for full-time study, prior to the examination.

3. *Open learning courses.* More and more of these courses are being promoted, extending up to the academic level of MBA. The structure is similar to that described in 2 above with a period of intensive full-time study at the end. Progress in part-time studies is monitored regularly and evaluated by self-administered testing procedures, coupled with postal tuition. Some courses incorporate interactive video teaching.

Whatever training strategy is adopted it is important to remember that training courses are not the only methods by which employees learn new skills, acquire knowledge and change attitudes. Contributions are made by:

- Planned reading.
- Programmed instruction.
- Counselling.
- Attendance at particular meetings.

- Project work.
- Planned visits to factories, exhibitions, and suppliers.
- Job rotation.
- Temporary secondment.

The training adjuncts can be shown in the training plan, which will show the training strategy to be adopted and the methods of implementation. The full structure will include:

- Training needs.
- Methods by which the needs will be met.
- A schedule of training and non-training activities.
- The persons responsible for carrying out training and other activities.
- The methods of evaluating success or failure of the training programme.

## Fresh Horizons
### *Question: What is NVQ — how does it help?*

From its low position in the world training league tables Britain is fighting back. A National Council for Vocational Qualifications has been established. The concept of NVQs (National Vocational Qualifications) is all about doing a job well. An NVQ is a kitemark. The National Council for Vocational Qualifications (NCVQ) accredits the NVQ awards for England, Northern Ireland and Wales, although it does not award them. NVQs are awarded by established bodies such as City & Guilds, BTEC and the RSA. In Scotland, the sole awarding body is Scotvec, which is also responsible for accrediting Scottish Vocational Qualifications (SVQs). The National Council for Vocational Qualifications oversees and co-ordinates the NVQ operation. Information and publicity is readily available from the Council; the address is NCVQ, 222 Euston Road, London NW1 2BZ (Tel. 071-387 9898). Information is also available locally from all TECs (Training and Enterprise Councils).

NVQ represents a positive implemented effort, initiated by the government in 1986, to achieve standards of work competence that have been pre-set by industry and commerce. The entire workforce is covered: NVQs span all sectors and all levels of the workforce. A positive target has been set by the Confederation of British Industry of 12 million NVQ certificates to be issued by 1996.

Each NVQ is made up of a number of separate units. These units set out precisely what the candidate must be able to do and to what standard. An NVQ framework embraces all NVQs according to their occupational area, with five levels of achievement. Level 1 is the simplest level — 'competence in the performance of a range of varied work activities' — and the levels rise to the professional standards of level 5 — 'application of a significant range of fundamental principles and complex techniques across a wide variety of contexts; substantial personal autonomy; acceptability for analysis and diagnosis, design, planning execution and evaluation'.

Full details of the National Vocational Qualifications Framework is available on the computerized National Database. This database is helpful to trainers for planning with candidates and developing action programmes. It is emphasized that NVQ per se is not a training programme, but a qualification.

The Training and Enterprise Councils use the National Database in conjunction with the National Record. This has four sections:

- The personal record, giving the individual's experience.
- An Action Plan, showing career plans and training targets.
- Assessment Record, documenting progress towards those targets.
- Qualifications, showing NVQs and credits already achieved.

The information provided by the National Record is helpful to employers in providing an instant profile of an applicant's achievements.

From the point of view of employers NVQ is an excellent practical concept because the qualifications of skills and knowledge are based on national standards developed by industry. Across the country Industry Lead Bodies are developing the industry-defined standards of competence. In many cases, qualifications are created where no previous qualification existed within the occupation.

From the students' side NVQ is a plus too. There are no barriers of age or previous education, and there are no time limits. As the NVQ is a measure of what the individual can do, work for the qualification can be undertaken on the job, as well as at college or in the student's own time. Existing job experience borne of many years at work counts because credits are given for all relevant personal competence.

## Summary

*Question:* In an organization, what added-value benefits are derived from the training function?

*Answer:* Training enhances progress through a range of added-value benefits. They are: increased production, fewer industrial accidents, heightened job satisfaction, reduced labour turnover, staff retention, generating a positive public image, and the creation of an awareness amongst all staff of the customer as No. 1.

*Question:* How are training needs assessed at organizational level?
*Answer:* There are four stages in the assessment of organizational training needs: (1) setting audit objectives and the terms of reference; (2) gathering information; (3) preparing recommendations; (4) procedures for implementation. The process can be made difficult by managers feeling threatened or seeking political sway.

*Question:* How are individual training needs assessed?
*Answer:* In assessing individual training needs, the opinion of the line manager is first sought. The job is then analysed into its component tasks, sub-tasks and elements.

*Question:* What are the major training strategies?
*Answer:* The major training strategies are: (1) induction training; (2) on-the-job training; (3) off-the-job training; (4) external training; (5) in-house training.

*Question:* What is NVQ: how does it help?
*Answer:* NVQ is the National Vocational Qualification – it is a kitemark, recognisable as a qualification of competence at work, independent of any educational grade. Each NVQ is made up of a number of separate units and there is a framework of five levels of achievement. Because NVQs span all sectors of the national workforce, the NVQ project makes a positive contribution to upgrading nationally current levels of training in industry and commerce.

# 5

# BUILDING BETTER EMPLOYEE RELATIONS

Before reading this chapter answer the following questions concerned with helping employees to perform well. The questions are worked through in the text. Questions and answers are given together at the end of the chapter as a summary.

## Questions

- What options exist in respect of employee working hours?
- What preparations are advisable before an employer changes working hours?
- What are the key elements of a payments policy for employees?
- What systems of performance-related pay enhance employee performance?
- What pay schemes other than direct payment by results enhance employee performance?
- What elements must be considered prior to implementing a job evaluation pay scheme?
- What is the relevance of salary surveys to the enhancement of employee performance?

## Choosing the Best Work Day

***Question: What options exist in respect of employee working hours?***

In the 1990s the issue of hours of work is high on the agenda for both employers and employees. For the employer the issue is clear: the introduction of new technologies, scheduled to provide future benefits, frequently demand intensive 'teething trouble' attention and extra hours. In the retail sections of industry, requirements are growing to provide more hours available to the public as part of immaculate customer service. Employees must work harder and longer.

For employees the perspective is different. The trends are fewer working hours, more leisure time. This is particularly so for women, wanting to work hours to fit in with their domestic arrangements. In support, unions are pursuing claims for 35-hour working weeks.

The European Union is currently considering a directive on working time. Clearly hours of work is a key to the success of the employer and to the job satisfaction of the employee.

There are a number of options for mutually acceptable agreements over working hours between employer and employee.

### *Part-time working*

In the last decade part-time working has increased significantly. Employers are using part-time workers, in day shifts or evening shifts, to meet peak demands. Mostly this labour is female. An increasing number of retired people are offering their labour on a part-time basis. Also increasing is the volume of students available to work weekends and in the vacations. Because of the growing sources of part-time labour, employers have the attractive option of reducing their full-time labour force, knowing that they can meet additional labour requirements with part-time staff. The option is attractive because although labour rates for part-time workers are not significantly cheaper, unproductive time is not paid for.

Care must be taken with employment of female part-time labour, so that the terms offered do not lead to claims against discrimination. Another constraint is that the use of part-time labour leads to higher labour turnover with increased recruitment and training costs. Because of this part-time labour supply is normally restricted to lower-skilled jobs. Within this category, experienced workers with young children or other domestic commitments are encouraged to return on a part-time basis.

Many of the major UK retailers are now moving to employing part-time staff to meet the requirements of extended daily opening and Sunday working. The availability of part-time staff allows them great flexibility in meeting their peak and low sales periods during opening hours.

### *Job sharing*

Job sharing is another form of part-time work. Here two employees share the responsibility for one full-time job. The work is split into alternative days or alternative weeks, or whichever other arrangement is mutually convenient.

Generally there is a requirement that additional working is expected from both job sharers to meet peak demands; in such cases both may be at work at the same time. It is expected that one sharer covers for the absence of the other.

The arrangement works well when both sharers have similar qualifications and experience, and where both sharers get on well together. Problems can sometimes arise when one job sharer leaves and it is difficult to find a replacement.

### *Flexible working hours*

Flexible working hours, also known as 'flexitime', is an arrangement whereby the working period relates to a given number of hours falling within a certain time. Employees choose when to begin and when to end their working day within a range of hours, provided they are present during a core time. Some arrangements also provide that if at the end of a specified period of weeks or months, employees have worked more hours than required, the additional hours can be taken subsequently as leave of absence or 'flexi-leave'.

An example of flexi-time is shown below:

08.00 — 10.00: Flexible starting time
10.00 — 12.00: Core working time (everyone is present)
12.00 — 14.00: Flexible lunch-time
14.00 — 16.00: Core working time
16.00 — 18.00: Flexible finishing time

Employees required to work 7.5 hours per day with a one-hour lunch break can vary the start and finish times, and the lunch break, provided they are at work during the core times of 10.00-12.00 and 14.00-16.00.

The advantage of flexitime is the freedom given to employees to organize their working hours to match their personal needs. This is particularly advantageous for avoiding rush-hour traffic and for those with childcare responsibilities. The system works well in organizations that employ large numbers of people, ensuring cover at all times yet allowing employees to work at times to suit their preference. Disadvantages are that supervision is not always available, and heating and lighting costs are higher because of the longer day. For this system employees are required to record their start and finish times and a method of time recording may need to be introduced, adding a further overhead.

### Compressed working week

When production economics warrant, many employers opt for a reduction in the working week. There are a variety of working patterns — for example:

- 4½-day weeks.
- 4-day weeks.
- 9-day fortnights.
- 9½-day fortnights.
- 6-day fortnights.

The principle is a reallocation of working time into fewer but longer days during the week. The arrangements are beneficial to the employer by reducing the number of start-ups, reducing factory overheads, reducing overtime, labour turnover and absenteeism. The benefits to the employees are longer weekends, with increased leisure opportunities.

A typical example was in a flour-packing plant. Staff worked a five-day week: Mondays to Thursday 7.30 am — 4.30 pm and Fridays 7.30 am — 11.30 am, with a half-hour lunch break Mondays to Thursdays. The trade union was agitating for a 37.5-hour working week. Management rejected the claim, but agreement was reached on a four-day working week of 7.30 am to 5.30 pm with a 30-minute lunch break. With this arrangement management maintained a 38-hour working week, but saved on the Friday start-up and clean-down costs. The union achieved no reduction in working hours for its members, but was happy with the benefit of a three-day weekend.

There are certain constraints imposed by the compressed working week on work that is particularly demanding physically or mentally. The longer working day may affect the health and safety of the employee.

### Annualized hours contracts

Annualized hours contracts entail the calculation of working time on an annual basis rather than a weekly or monthly basis. 'Annual hours' are used to harmonize the hours employees work when different levels of production are required within a year.

An example is in the manufacture of milk and cheese products.

There are both seasonal fluctuations and continuous process working requirements. The busiest times of the year are April, May, June and Christmas, with the summer months of August and September slack. Prior to the introduction of annualised hours, the manufacturers adopted a mixture of overtime payments plus the recruitment of temporary staff in the busy times, whilst staff were laid off in the slack periods. A problem that arose was employees devising less efficient working practices to protect their jobs and to fix the levels of overtime working.

When annualised hours salary payments were introduced, the need to create overtime work was eliminated. During peak periods employees worked a six-day week, and in slack periods a four-day week. The outcome of a change to annualised hours payment resulted in a change of employee attitude. Rigid overtime and job-related demarcations gave way to a more positive and flexible attitude built on job security and predictability of earnings.

For employers the attraction of an annualised hours contract is clear-cut. It is the elimination of overtime and the ability to match working hours to peaks and lulls in production. For employees, the principal benefits include improved basic pay and periods when there are fewer hours at work. Many employers take advantage of annualised hours contracts to introduce, at the same time, new payment systems and working practices. Terms and conditions are harmonized to provide salaried status for all employees.

For a number of high overtime workers annualised hours contracts result in a reduction in pay, which may need to be offset by a phased reduction of hours in the period leading up to the change in payment system. Another option is for the high overtime workers to be made a one-off payment reflecting the short-term loss of income that will be incurred.

The following example illustrates how annual hours are calculated:

| | | |
|---|---|---|
| Basic working week | | 39 hours |
| Working day (39 divided by 5) | | 7.8 hours |
| Annual holidays | | 25 days |
| Statutory holidays | | 8 days |
| Total hours in a year (52.2 × 39)[1] | | = 2036 |
| Less annual holidays (25 × 7.8) | = 195 | |
| Less statutory holidays (8 × 7.8) | = 62 | |
| | 257 | (257) |
| Annual hours | | 1779 |

[1]Union negotiations have established the precedent of calculating an annual number of weeks based on a leap year cycle.

In addition to the basic annual hours employers may add additional hours required to meet business demands. The basic annual hours, plus additional hours if required, would be the maximum number of hours required to be worked by the employee. The employee's individual contract then specifies when those hours are to be worked during the year. Irrespective of the hours subsequently worked, employees are paid an annual salary, monthly in arrears. It is in the employee's interest to work efficiently and reduce absenteeism in order to minimize the need to work any additional hours.

For continuous process production involving continuous shift work of 24 hours per day, seven days a week, 52 weeks per year, a five-crew system is normally employed. An annual rota is established for four of the crews, incorporating rest days, morning, evening and night shifts. The remaining crew provides cover for planned and unplanned absences. An example of a five-crew system is shown below:

| | Mon | Tues | Wed | Thurs | Fri | Sat | Sun |
|---|---|---|---|---|---|---|---|
| Week 1 | AM | PM | N | R | R | AM | PM |
| Week 2 | N | R | R | AM | PM | N | R |
| Week 3 | R | AM | PM | N | R | R | AM |
| Week 4 | AM | N | R | R | AM | PM | N |
| Week 5 | R | R | AM | PM | N | R | R |

where AM = 6.00 am to 2.00 pm
PM = 2.00 pm to 10.00 pm
N = 10.00 pm to 6.00 am
R = Rest day

For seasonal working, longer hours are worked in one period, and shorter in the other. For example, a local authority Parks Department works 45 hours per week for 30 weeks in the summer and 30.75 hours per week the rest of the year.

## Essential Planning

***Question: What preparations are advisable before an employer changes working hours?***

Careful planning before the introduction of changes to working hours is essential. The impact of change to production systems, manning levels, absence control procedures, communication procedures and employees' contracts of employment invariably disrupts the status quo. Morale becomes low. Efficiency and output drop.

Consultation with managers, trade unions or employee representatives must precede action. A working party should be set up with the task of planning, implementing and monitoring the desired changes in working hours. If there is no in-house experience on which to call, it is advisable to instruct an outside expert. The project can be undertaken by a firm of management consultants. Employers contemplating change must reinforce a smooth transition by creating effective communication channels.

Full information must be passed to employees and important feedback gained.

It is a legal requirement that the consent of employees is obtained before any changes are introduced to employees' contracts of employment.

## Practical Ways to Pay

***Question: What are the key elements of a payments policy for employees?***

A fair salary and wages policy are key elements in enhancing employee performance. Basic wages and salary on their own are unlikely to enhance performance but performance-related pay systems have been found to provide considerable motivation to individual performance. An unfair wages and salary system certainly leads to disgruntled employees. It is strongly recommended that companies with more than fifty employees establish a salary and wages policy and communicate it to their employees.

Many employers in the United Kingdom operate two payment systems: a salaried system for 'white-collar' workers and a wage system for 'blue-collar' jobs. In such cases two different policy statements are required, although following the Wages Act, 1986, there is increasing overlap.

A number of important elements must be included within a salary policy and a wages policy. These are given separately below.

### *Salary policy statement*

- A clear statement of the company's objectives.
- The salary structure is based on a form of job evaluation. Each job has a salary range with a declared minimum and maximum salary.
- Details of the job evaluation system used.
- The criteria by which an employee's initial salary is determined.

- Criteria for performance appraisal.
- Details of any performance-related payment.
- Basis for salary review — e.g. over the age of eighteen, all staff salaries are reviewed annually.
- Details of payment on change of grade.
- Basis for progression within salary range — e.g. good performance in the job permits the maximum of the salary range to be reached in four years and staff already on their salary ceiling will be subject to a salary review every third year, to a maximum of six years.
- Grievance procedure to be followed for any employee with a salary grievance.

## *Wages policy*

- A clear statement of the company's objectives.
- The basis for the wage structure on a form of job evaluation. Generally, there is mutual agreement between management and unions for job evaluation to be carried out on a joint basis.
- Details of the job evaluation system used.
- The rate for the job — no one is paid less than the rate for the job. Notwithstanding the right of the unions' joint negotiating panel to negotiate on behalf of its members, management philosophy is to link rates to company progress.
- Details of the wages structure.
- Number of grades. The differential between grades should realistically reflect differences in responsibility and skills.
- How the incentive payments system works.
- Details of minimum earnings — e.g. no employee will receive less than £100 for a 40-hour week.
- The basis for payment on promotion — e.g. on promotion the employee takes the rate for the job, but when the employee is already on maximum earnings for his grade there is a probationary period of three months at the old rate prior to establishment at the new grade.
- How the incentive payment system works.
- Payment with changes of grade.
- Grievance procedure.
- Agreements with the joint negotiating panel.

## Valuable Options

### *Question: What systems of performance-related pay enhance employee performance?*

Is it fair to pay all employees the same amount, when individual performances or group performances differ? Traditionally, the majority of employers pay employees on a time rate system expressed as an hourly rate, a weekly wage or an annual salary, paid in twelve equal instalments.

Such systems are easy to implement, easy to monitor and clearly understood by employees. However, time rates offer little encouragement for the improvement of individual performance, efficiency or productivity.

There is a range of performance-related pay systems available to employers that can be used for all types of employment. Traditionally, in the United Kingdom, annual pay reviews reflect the rate of inflation rather than company performance. Often, linked with pay reviews, prices are increased to accommodate pay awards or lower margins are accepted arising from increased labour costs. Sometimes labour is reduced to control wage and salary costs. The introduction of a performance-related pay scheme is a method of assisting companies to reduce the need for pay increases that are simply in line with inflation or inflation plus. The reason is that well-managed performance-related pay systems result in improved efficiency and productivity. The result is financial benefit to the employer and an opportunity that did not exist before for employees to improve earnings by improving performance.

Various performance-related pay systems are considered below:

### *Payments by results (PBR)*

PBR has application to individuals or to groups of employees. There are different variations of the scheme but in the main payment by results is linked fully, or partially, to performance. The best form of payment by results is on an individual basis whereby the individual's level of output is measured over a set period. Three common forms of payment by results are:

- *Piecework.* The employee is paid a rate per unit of output. For example, a bricklayer is paid a rate for each brick laid.
- *Standard time system.* A set standard time is allowed to complete a particular task. The employee is then paid according to the time allowed for each task. Time taken in excess of the standard time results in lower pay, and time taken less than standard time, in higher pay.

- *Commission.* Commission as a form of payments by results is generally used for sales performance. Additional payments are made in relation to the value of sales and/or profits that are achieved.

When PBR schemes are applicable to groups the bonus element is divided among the group employees to an agreed proportion. The groups work as a team. Each member performs similar or complementary jobs. The smaller the group the more effective the system.

Most PBR schemes use the British Standards Institution scale where a '75' performance equates with a non-incentive level and a '100' performance is the standard of performance an employee on a PBR scheme is projected to achieve. Empirical data and personal observation support the view that a financially motivated employee produces one third more output than a financially unmotivated worker.

A PBR scheme of one third extra effort above the norm resulting in one third extra payment is known as a 'straight-line proportional payment by results' scheme. The principle is that, subject to any guaranteed minimum, earnings vary in the same proportion as performance, i.e. for every 1 per cent movement in performance above or below standard performance, earnings change in the same proportion.

There are other schemes where performance and earnings relate differently:

- Progressive schemes where the rate of change in earnings rises as performance rises.
- Regressive schemes in which the rate of change in earnings falls as performance rises.
- Geared schemes where a bonus payment extrapolated below the minimum earnings level does not give zero earnings at zero performance.
- Stabilized schemes where a bonus extended below the minimum earnings level gives some earnings at zero performance.

Sometimes two of these schemes are used in combination, changing from one scheme to the other, at predetermined levels of performance. Figure 5.1 gives a comparison of the various PBR schemes.

The most common form of payments by results scheme is the straight-line method. In introducing such a scheme the first step, using work measurement techniques would be to determine the standard time for a job, expressing this in standard minutes. For example, if a job has a value of five standard minutes, 40 completed jobs have a work value of 200 standard minutes, irrespective of the time taken to complete the job.

An employee within an 8-hour day may spend 7.5 hours on PBR work and is capable, therefore, of completing 90 jobs at 5 minutes. The achievement is standard performance and earning time rate plus 33.3 per cent. If, however, only 80 jobs were completed in 7.5 hours the employee performance would be:

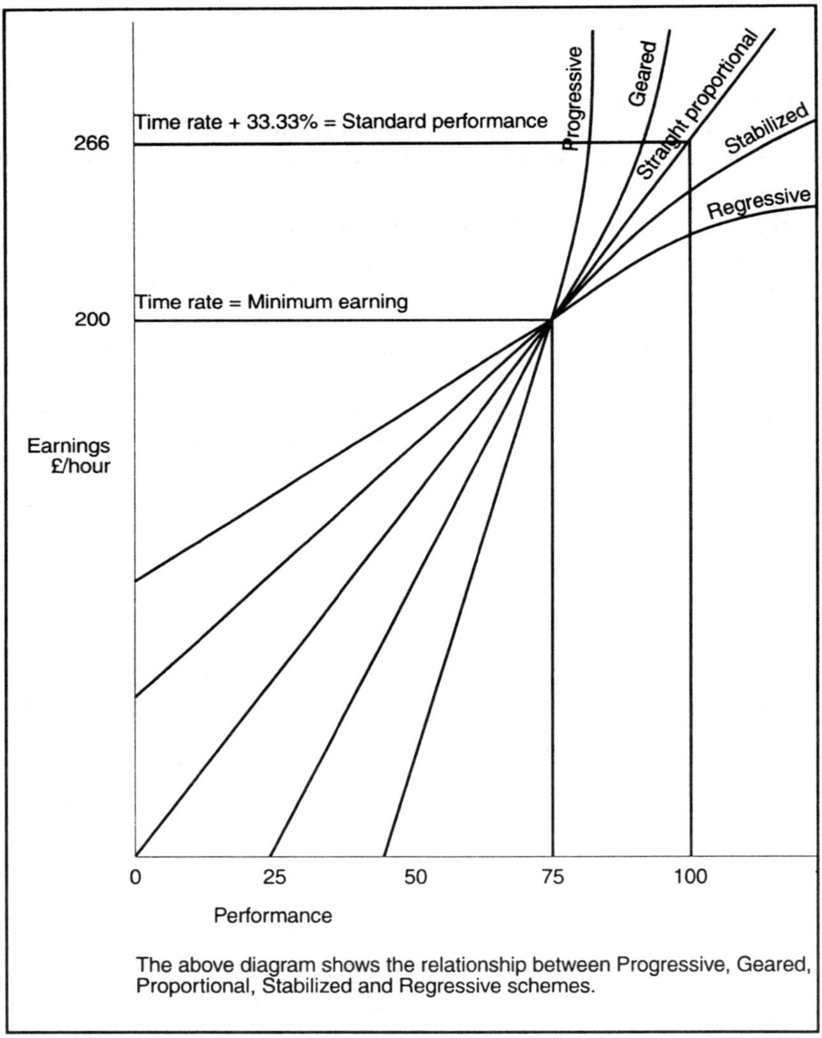


*Figure 5.1. Comparison of 'Payment by results' (PBR) schemes.*

$$\frac{80}{90} \times 100 = 88.8\%$$

If 100 jobs are completed in 7.5 hours the employee performance is:

$$\frac{100}{90} \times 100 = 111\%$$

*Bonus earnings*

Assume £2 = Standard time rate.

If 90 jobs are completed, rate = 100% + 33.33% = £2.66

If 80 jobs are completed, rate = 88.8% of £2.66 = £2.37

If 100 jobs are completed, rate = 111% of £2.66 = £2.96

Total earnings would be 30 minutes at £2 per hour, i.e. £1 plus bonus earnings per hour × 7.5.

Payment by results systems are best used where it is possible to measure work and attribute this directly to the individual, rather than to a machine or process. Of necessity, for the systems to work well there must be sufficient work available to allow bonus payments to be earned.

Standards of performance are significant. They are determined by using work measurement techniques. The two most common methods are:

- *Work study method.* The techniques of method study and work measurement are used to give employees a defined basis of operation within a standard time. Employees are timed in the performance of their tasks, accounting for their different rates of working.
- *Predetermined motion time systems.* Standards are set using predetermined data. Where new tasks are involved, they are broken down into measurable elements. The measurements are then assembled into new standards for the new tasks.

## Measured day work

In measured day work pay is set at a level higher than normal time rate on the condition that the employee maintains a consistent level of performance. Stepped measured day work is the situation where a number of performance levels operate, each carrying a differing rate of pay related to performance. This allows employees to increase their work rate to move to higher rates of pay. For those employees whose work rate falls, payment drops to the lower rates. For measured day work to be successful, there must be good management control, effective supervision and a developed sense of teamwork. In addition, the labour force must be flexible and able to maintain a steady work flow.

### *Plant and company-wide schemes*

Plant and company-wide schemes are payment schemes that allow all production workers or all employees to participate in a bonus scheme. In its simplest form, a company manufacturing one type of product may have a scheme based directly on the total volume of output. Historical records over, say, the previous year determine output per man-hour. Any increase in output per man-hour results in a saving of wages over the previous period. Such savings are then shared between employees and the company to an agreed formula.

Where companies produce a range of products, an 'added value' system may be adopted. Added value is sales revenue less expenditure on materials and services purchased outside the company. The figure remaining is the value added within the company, consisting of internal business costs and profit. The level of added value is an indicator of efficiency. Therefore any increase in added value above the norm is regarded as an improvement in performance. Savings generated by an improvement in added value are divided in an agreed proportion between employees and the company. An example of the added value scheme is as follows:

*Calculation of norm*

| | £ |
|---|---|
| Sales revenue over 3-year performance period | 5,000,000 |
| Less bought in materials and services | 3,000,000 |
| Added value over 3 years | 2,000,000 |

Employee costs over 3 years = £500,000

Ratio of employee costs to added value:

$$\frac{500{,}000}{2{,}000{,}000} \times 100 = 25\%$$

*Bonus calculation*

| | | |
|---|---|---|
| Sales revenue over 1 month, say | 150,000 | |
| Less bought in materials and service | 90,000 | |
| Added value | 60,000 | |
| 25% of added value | | 15,000 |
| Less employee costs | | 14,000 |
| Saving available for distribution | | £1,000 |

60%, say, of the saving is paid to employees — employee share is equal to:

$$\frac{£600}{£14{,}000} \times 100 = 4.28\%$$

This type of scheme works well where management and the workforce are willing to cooperate fully, where there is good understanding and where two-way communication channels between management and the workforce are well established.

### *Profit sharing*

In profit-sharing schemes employees receive a bonus dependent upon the size of profit, above an agreed level, in the previous accounting period. The bonus may be paid in cash, in shares or both. The scheme aims to promote interest in the overall performance of the company and seeks to gain improved employee performance.

The government, in wishing to encourage profit-related schemes, have introduced tax incentives whereby profit-related payment up to a maximum of £4,000 or 20 per cent of pay is non-taxable. Inland Revenue rules and regulations must be adhered to and all schemes need to be registered with the tax authorities. Latest statistics indicate that around 3,000 schemes are in existence covering three quarters of a million employees and, providing the tax incentive remains, it is expected that this number will increase significantly.

### *Performance-rating pay schemes*

A performance-rating pay scheme links payment to the individual performance of an employee assessed by a systematic and fair appraisal scheme. (See Chapter 8 for Performance Appraisal.) Payments are made either as a lump-sum payment or as supplementary payments. A disadvantage of cumulative supplementary payments is that they can create embarrassing differences in payment between employees doing similar jobs, and they have little relationship to market rates.

The lump-sum payment is generally considered the best form of payment. It clearly gives the payment an identity of its own, and the lump sum can be paid at popular times, such as Christmas or before the summer holidays. Most companies pay performance payments related to the overall performance of the employee. A typical scheme ranks the overall performance in one of five levels:

Level A: Achieves considerably more than required by the job.
Level B: More than meets the requirements of the job.
Level C: Meets the requirements of the job.
Level D: Fails to meet some requirements of the job.
Level E: Fails to meet the requirements of the job.

Alternatively these levels could be determined as:

| | | *Weighting factor* |
|---|---|---|
| A | Excellent | 10 |
| B | Good | 7.5 |
| C | Satisfactory | 5 |
| D | Fair | 2.5 |
| E | Poor | 0 |

As illustrated, a weighting factor is applied to each level and the total unit calculated. The amount of money to be allocated to performance payment is then divided by the numbers of the units, giving the payment per unit. An example is illustrated below.

| *Level units* | *Unit value* | *No. of employees* | *Total* |
|---|---|---|---|
| A | 10 | 20 | 200 |
| B | 7.5 | 40 | 300 |
| C | 5 | 140 | 700 |
| D | 2.5 | 30 | 75 |
| E | 0 | 20 | 0 |
| | | Total | 1,275 |

Amount of money available for payment (2.5% pay bill) = £63,750

$$\text{Value per unit} = \frac{£63{,}750}{1{,}275} = £50$$

Bonus payment therefore:

| | | |
|---|---|---|
| Level | A | £500 |
| | B | £375 |
| | C | £250 |
| | D | £125 |
| | E | nil |

There is some merit in companies considering performance payments the sole criteria for annual pay increases instead of the traditional Retail Price Index links. This method is often used with the total amount split between a proportion consolidated into the employee basic wage and the balance paid as an annual bonus.

***Skills-based pay schemes***

Another method of improving employee effectiveness is to introduce a skills-based pay scheme. Specific levels of pay are linked to different levels of task. As the complexity of the task increases so the levels of pay increase. The employer provides the training for the employee to achieve a higher level of skill, carrying a higher rate of pay, but this is done outside of normal working hours. The employee is not paid for the extra hours of training, but takes advantage of the opportunity for self-development provided by the employer.

## Belt and Braces

***Question: What pay schemes other than direct payment by results enhance employee performance?***

Job evaluation is a process whereby different jobs are evaluated using the same yardstick to produce a ranking order of jobs. The yardstick is the first step in establishing a fair and equitable payment system designed to motivate staff to achieve good performance. There are a number of ways to evaluate jobs, some simple, some complex. The four main techniques are described below.

***Job ranking***

Job ranking is the simplest of the evaluation techniques. A number of 'key' jobs are chosen which cover the whole range of jobs. A job description is prepared for each 'key' job describing duties, responsibilities and the qualifications required. These key jobs are then ranked in an order reflecting the degree of complexity, responsibility, and difficulty.

The remaining jobs are compared against the key jobs and inserted appropriately in the ranking scale, providing a full ranking scale for all company jobs. Finally, the ranking scale is divided into a number of grades. Each grade has a number of jobs of approximately similar content.

### *Paired comparison*

Paired comparison is another variation of job ranking that is commonly used. Where the number of jobs to be evaluated is small, i.e. 20—30 jobs, all of the jobs are evaluated. Where the number is greater, key jobs will again need to be identified, ranked and the remaining jobs, similar to key jobs, inserted in the ranking.

Under paired comparison each job is compared with every other job, in turn. If a job is considered more important, two points are awarded; if equally important, one point; and if less important, no points. This process is carried out independently by several assessors using common job descriptions. The sum of the assessors' job points produces the job ranking. As with job ranking, after the master ranking has been obtained, the ranking scale is divided into grades. The process of paired comparison is refined by calculating a coefficient of agreement between assessors which should be greater than 0.75. If it is less, assessors are required to re-examine their assessment. Figure 5.2 illustrates an example of paired comparison.

### *Job classification*

Here the number of grades under job classification are decided in advance. Each grade has recognizable characteristics, taking into account discernable differences in skill and responsibility required by the jobs in that grade. Job descriptions are then prepared for each job, and jobs are allocated to the predetermined grades. An example is given below.

- *Grade A.* Tasks are easy to perform and follow laid-down procedures. The position is constantly supervised and work is frequently checked.
- *Grade B.* Tasks follow laid-down procedures but a limited amount of initiative is required. Supervision is always available and the work is subject to spot checks. (Up to three months' training required.)

- *Grade C.* Tasks are carried out and decisions made with reference to standard procedures. Regular contact with own-level staff to obtain

| | Accounts clerk | Wages clerk | Secretary | Shorthand typist | Typist | Sales clerk | Telephonist | Receptionist | VDU operator | Accounts supervisor | Total points |
|---|---|---|---|---|---|---|---|---|---|---|---|
| Accounts clerk | X | 0 | 0 | 0 | 1 | 0 | 0 | 0 | 0 | 0 | 1 |
| Wages clerk | 2 | X | 0 | 1 | 2 | 1 | 1 | 1 | 1 | 0 | 9 |
| Secretary | 2 | 2 | X | 2 | 2 | 2 | 2 | 2 | 2 | 0 | 16 |
| Shorthand typist | 2 | 1 | 0 | X | 2 | 1 | 1 | 1 | 1 | 0 | 9 |
| Typist | 1 | 0 | 0 | 0 | X | 0 | 0 | 0 | 0 | 0 | 1 |
| Sales Clerk | 2 | 1 | 0 | 1 | 2 | X | 1 | 1 | 0 | 0 | 8 |
| Telephonist | 2 | 1 | 0 | 1 | 2 | 1 | X | 1 | 0 | 0 | 8 |
| Receptionist | 2 | 1 | 0 | 1 | 2 | 1 | 1 | X | 0 | 0 | 8 |
| VDU operator | 2 | 1 | 0 | 1 | 2 | 2 | 2 | 2 | X | 0 | 12 |
| Accounts supervisor | 2 | 2 | 2 | 2 | 2 | 2 | 2 | 2 | 2 | X | 18 |

*Job ranking*

| | | |
|---|---|---|
| Accounts supervisor | 18 | Grade 1 |
| Secretary | 16 | |
| VDU operator | 12 | Grade 2 |
| Shorthand typist | 9 | Grade 3 |
| Wages clerk | 9 | |
| Sales clerk | 8 | |
| Telephonist | 8 | |
| Receptionist | 8 | |
| Accounts clerk | 1 | Grade 4 |
| Typist | 1 | |

*Figure 5.2. A paired comparison analysis form.*

and provide information. Occasional supervision is necessary. (Minimum two years' experience required.)

- *Grade D.* After direction the employee plans and arranges work with little or no supervision. Requires contact with higher-level staff and external personnel to obtain and receive information that may be confidential. (Minimum four years' experience required.)

### *Points rating*

Points rating is a commonly used job evaluation technique. It is a method that breaks each job down into a number of factors — e.g. skill, responsibility, effort and working conditions. These factors are often further broken down into degrees or levels, with points allocated. The following table shows an example of a points rating scheme:

| Factors | 1st Degree | 2nd Degree | 3rd Degree | 4th Degree | 5th Degree |
|---|---|---|---|---|---|
| Skill: | | | | | |
| Education | 14 | 28 | 42 | 56 | 70 |
| Experience | 26 | 52 | 78 | 105 | 130 |
| Effort: | | | | | |
| Physical | 10 | 20 | 30 | 40 | 50 |
| Dexterity | 10 | 20 | 0 | 40 | 50 |
| Mental | 10 | 20 | 30 | 40 | 50 |
| Responsibility: | | | | | |
| Equipment | 5 | 10 | 15 | 20 | 25 |
| Material | 5 | 10 | 15 | 20 | 25 |
| Safety | 5 | 10 | 15 | 20 | 25 |
| Working conditions: | 15 | 30 | 45 | 60 | 75 |

A total points figure for each employee is then calculated by adding the tally for each of the separate factors. Under this scheme the maximum number of points available is set, say, at 500. Job descriptions are prepared for each job, describing the job in terms of the points factors. From the completed points factor list of all jobs, grades are then set. One method of determining the weighting of each factor is to use the paired comparison method described above.

## Taking Precautions

***Question: What elements must be considered prior to implementing a job evaluation pay scheme?***

There are a number of considerations that influence the smooth running of a job evaluation pay scheme.

*Available in-house expertise.* Firms without personnel departments are advised to seek expert advice before proceeding. Sources of advice are management consultants or the Advisory Conciliation and Arbitration Service (ACAS).

*Discrimination.* Extreme care is necessary that no discrimination, direct or indirect, can be construed from the design and operation of the scheme. If external professional help is not sought, it may be advisable to ask ACAS to validate the company scheme.

*Commitment.* Total commitment is necessary for a job evaluation pay scheme to work. The full support of management, employees and trade unions is required before any scheme is implemented.

*Participation.* Job evaluation lends itself to joint participation, and successful job evaluation schemes invariably involve management and employee representatives. It is normal for a steering committee to be established to consider policy issues and to oversee the job evaluation exercise. A job evaluation committee of no more than eight is best to represent all groups of employees. Members of the committee should possess in-depth knowledge of the range of jobs to be evaluated.

*Communication.* It is essential that all employees are kept informed of the method of job evaluation being used, and the timescale. Employees should be given up-to-date progress reports, and the results of the completed study.

*Protection of existing pay.* Job evaluation may lead to some employees' jobs being placed in a lower grade that does not equate with their current pay. Prior to commencing job evaluation it is necessary to reach agreement on how to deal with this situation. The normal method is for the existing employee's pay rate to be retained as a personal rate — this is commonly known as 'red circling'.

In addition to the above considerations it is advisable to be aware of the 'equal pay' issue. Both European and UK law provide that in employment a woman has the right to treatment equal to that given to a man (a) on work of the same, or broadly similar, nature to that of a man and (b) in a job that, although different from that of a man, has been rated equivalent to the man's job under a job evaluation scheme.

Although it is common for women to claim equal pay, the right equally applies to men to claim equal pay against women. Most claims for equal pay are resolved without reference to the law, but claims can be made through Employment Appeal Tribunals. At such tribunals any defence using a job evaluation scheme must show the scheme to be analytical. Of the schemes discussed above only the points rating scheme is accepted as being analytical.

## Double Check

***Question: What is the relevance of salary surveys to the enhancement of employee performance?***

After carrying out job evaluations, and after jobs have been classified into their grades, it is most important that the decision-making is seen to be fair. It is necessary that within the company the relative worth of each job is equitable, and externally the wages reflect market rates.

Failure to maintain pay competitively with market rates will lead to loss of staff and difficulty in recruiting new staff. It is therefore important that salary surveys are carried out regularly, particularly when a new salary structure is introduced.

There are a number of ways to conduct such salary surveys.

- *Purchasing wage/salary surveys.* A number of organizations publish surveys on a regular basis at national and local level, covering a range of occupations.
- *Monitoring job applications.* The monitoring of wages and salaries paid to job applicants assists in determining occupational rates of pay. This is particularly useful when there are large numbers of applicants.
- *Monitoring advertised positions.* Careful records of advertised wages and salaries for positions similar to those in the company give an indication of market rates. However, it must be remembered that advertised figures do not always equate with the actual rates paid.
- *Membership of a salary club.* Salary clubs exist for members to exchange wage and salary information. Membership of the local club or an industry-based club provides comparisons with local and national salary/wage rates.

In addition to seeking wage and salary information it is important to determine what other employee benefits competitors are offering to form a total remuneration package. Comparison of job titles alone when gathering research data leads to many inaccuracies. It is advisable to compare job descriptions.

When researches are complete and the market rates and grading structure are seen to be realistic, the two aspects need to be reconciled with the company's ability to pay. The survey of market rates will produce a range of rates, and it is necessary to determine minimum, maximum and median rates, lower and upper quartiles, and average rates. From this analysis a company can determine where it wishes to be positioned in the market place, with reference to existing rates and the affordability of new rates.

In addition to payment of wages and salaries, many employees now look for additional employee benefits. To remain competitive, and to retain staff, employers are being put in the position where they must supply more and more benefits. All these have a cost to the employer that must be taken into account when costing employee remuneration packages. The most common benefits are as follows.

*Company cars.* For many managers the provision of a company car is a requirement of their employment. The value of having that car has to be quantified to ensure internal equity with managers for whom a car is not essential.

*Pension schemes.* In recent years the government has provided cash incentives to employers and employees to join private pension schemes. Many employees, particularly older employees, are well aware of the benefits of pension schemes.

*Sick pay schemes.* Most employees are attracted by the security of receiving payment when absent from work due to illness. Many schemes are service-related in that the longer the period of employment, the longer the period for which sick pay benefits are provided. Traditionally, the first three days of absence due to illness are not eligible for payment of sick pay, but the trend is now towards payment from day 1.

*Catering facilities.* Many larger employers provide on-site catering, usually offering meals at subsidized prices. For medium and smaller-sized companies, the provision of a rest room with some cooking facilities is a popular practice.

*Sports and social clubs.* Sports and social clubs are often organized in large companies. They can be greatly appreciated and much used by many of the employees. Other employers subsidize employee membership of public and private health and sports centres. For smaller companies, the organization of one-off events, such as Christmas parties and summer outings, is practical and popular.

*Company shops.* Where appropriate, company shops selling company products to employees at discounted prices are a valuable benefit.

*Creche facilities.* For companies employing large numbers of women, creche facilities are invaluable and can be the one single factor determining choice of employer. The facility may be relatively costly to provide but it is invariably balanced in value by opportunities for recruitment and the retention of female personnel.

## Summary

*Question:* What options exist in respect of employee working hours?

*Answer:* There are a number of options for working hours mutually acceptable to employee and employer. They are part-time working, job sharing, flexible working hours, the compressed working week, and annualised hours contracts.

*Question:* What preparations are advisable before an employer changes working hours?

*Answer:* The implications of change in working hours for employees are invariably dramatic. Morale suffers. Prior to change there must be full consultation with managers, trade unions and employee representatives. Liaison with experts experienced in the management of change is recommended.

*Question:* What are the key elements of a payments policy for employees?

*Answer:* In the UK a fair payments policy generally incorporates two payment systems: a salaried system for 'white-collar' workers and a wage system for 'blue-collar' workers. Performance-related pay systems provide valuable motivation to enhanced performance. Common to all payment systems is the requirement for full communication with employees in respect of system objectives, system structure, methods of implementation and the different criteria employed.

*Question:* What systems of performance-related pay enhance employee performance?

*Answer:* A range of performance-related pay systems is available to employers. This includes payments by results, measured day work, added-value schemes, profit-sharing, performance-rating pay schemes and skills-based pay schemes.

*Question:* What pay schemes other than direct payment by results enhance employee performance?

*Answer:* Pay schemes other than payment by results include job evaluation, job ranking, paired comparison, job classification and points rating.

*Question:* What elements must be considered prior to implementing a job evaluation pay scheme?

*Answer:* In a job evaluation pay scheme the considerations are: available in-house expertise; avoidance of discrimination; commitment of management, employees and trade unions; participation between management and employees; good communication; and protection of existing pay rates.

*Question:* What is the relevance of salary surveys to the enhancement of employee performance?

*Answer:* Salary surveys make a useful contribution to monitoring the fairness of pay schemes. Pay must be equitable within the company in terms of the relative worth of pay grades, and externally it must relate well to market rates. Salary surveys are conducted by: the purchase of published wage/salary surveys; monitoring job applications; monitoring advertised positions; and the membership of salary clubs.

# 6

# GETTING HELP FROM DESIGN

Before reading this chapter answer the following questions. The questions are discussed in the text. At the end of the chapter questions and answers are collected together as a summary.

## Questions

- What happens when design is poor?
- What are the ingredients of good job design?
- How important are physical working conditions?
- How does well-designed communication enhance performance?

## Cause for Concern

***Question: What happens when 'design' is poor?***

Poor design has many dimensions. One aspect is in the product itself. Lord Weinstock of GEC, the story goes, was walking around a radio and television plant. He chatted with an operative screwing a back to a radio set to hold it in place. He asked whether it was necessary for the backing to be so thick. It was not: as a result the thickness of the backing board was reduced. Considerable material cost savings resulted. Further savings were achieved through the use of shorter copper screws.

Design in service is another aspect. In May 1979 an American Airlines wide-body DC10, manufactured by McDonnell Douglas, took off from Chicago airport bound for Los Angeles. Just at the moment of lift-off the engine in the left wing tore out of its mountings. The plane crashed. Passengers and crew, numbering 273 people, died. The investigators discovered that an L-shaped bracket securing the engine in place was cracked. Immediate investigation of other DC10 planes operating in the USA revealed other cracks in the L-shaped flanges. The certificate of airworthiness was temporarily withdrawn. Losses of revenue to airlines operating the DC10 plane were estimated at $8 million per day.

The McDonnell Douglas maintenance manual stipulated inspection of the engine mountings after 20,000 hours of flying. American Airlines complied with this requirement. But as part of the maintenance procedure the engine was required to be lifted up and removed from the wing. This procedure within the servicing schedule demanded an expensive 450 man-hours labour. The design of the maintenance procedures gave little recognition to the operator's need, in terms of generating revenue, to keep planes flying. American Airlines, keeping the aircraft manufacturer informed of what they were doing, found a method of short-circuiting the steps in the maintenance procedure. A form of mechanical cradle was devised, but as a result at some point the maintenance engineers worked with a clearance tolerance of barely one inch. Although many maintenance schedules had been completed without apparent problem, the investigators considered that damage to the brackets had caused the cracks to occur.

There was a ripple effect leading from the poor design and the resulting crash. McDonnell Douglas lost sales in the ensuing years and was knocked from its position as one of the leading aircraft manufacturers.

Nearer to home, poor design of plant and layout are frequently seen in factories. Component materials clutter up the aisles. Operatives leave their machines and walk long distances to collect specific tools or materials. The ideal of uninterrupted smooth work flow through the factory, with work stations, machinery, storage, and ancillary equipment strategically sited and interlinked, is often ignored.

Problems in the workplace also arise when there is lack of flexibility in the design of jobs. Jobs that are shaped to meet the requirements of technical processes without allowance for the human elements of the person performing the work, rarely function smoothly. A job content is specified: a worker is found to 'fit' the job. If there is little choice of the methods to be adopted or inadequate interaction with other workers, the symptoms of psychological stress are soon manifest. They are generally recognizable by absenteeism, industrial accidents, product quality deficiencies — but they are not neatly labelled as to why they occur.

## Four-and-Twenty Blackbirds

***Question: What are the ingredients of good job design?***

Good job design is about humanizing jobs. Happy employees are productive. The climate of a happy productive workforce is one of good employee relations. In considering job design it is essential that job holders themselves are involved in the process. Worker perception and attitudes fine-tune the structure provided by management. Important characteristics are:

- A clear goal requiring a degree of challenge.
- Introduction of variety in the range of skills used and the speed of work to be adopted.
- A degree of responsibility for output.
- Discretion in allocation of job tasks.
- Feedback on performance by self and other workers.
- Opportunities for increasing knowledge and skills within the employee's competence range.
- Provision of adequate resources for the job to be carried out.
- Involvement in decision-making of front-line matters.
- Contact with other employees.

Achieving good design is not usually a quick process. Businesses and organizations have an existing momentum. For whatever reason change is introduced there is invariably an adverse reaction; the workforce is comfortable with the status quo, because that is what they know. The proper approach to redesign is to reach agreement between the job holders and management in order to have the best fit between the employees and corporate objectives.

In redesigning jobs it is unlikely that all the desirable characteristics from the point of view of the employees are going to be achieved: there has to be some trade-off between desirable and less desirable. As a first approach to redesigning jobs, job holders and their managers should analyse jobs into the component tasks. These tasks are then described by the employee using one of the following criteria:

- Stressful
- Boring
- Interesting
- Frustrating
- Pointless
- Powerless
- Stimulating
- Tedious
- Satisfying
- Meaningful
- Responsible

In addition, the proportion of time spent by the job holder on each task is recorded. The responses are pointers to management for the direction of change. Change is likely to be appropriate not only in the job itself, but in the total environment in which the work takes place. What may need to go are some of the management constants — factors carved in the solid stones of 'them' and 'us'. Tom Peters says: 'I don't care if you've waited twenty-seven years for it, get rid of the damned reserved parking spot this bloody minute. Then you can consider asking "them" to "do it right first time".'

There are many examples of positive redesign in the management/job/environment milieu that do not cost a lot in terms of money or time:

- Clean toilets and cloakrooms.
- A clean, freshly painted communal dining room/canteen for management and staff together.
- Discretion to make customer service enhancing decisions without prior consultation.
- Removal of separate entrances for management and workers.

The focus is on empowering the workforce to think and act as an integral part of the company. There are managers and there are workers, but front-line workers have a real contribution to make in any decisions affecting how they work. It was not always so: in the early days managers knew best, though they did try hard to be creative in the ways that they knew.

F.W. Taylor, one of the pioneers of time and motion study, proposed a scientific approach to management. In his book published in 1911, he argued that a stopwatch and clipboard gave the most effective route to enhanced production. Worker activities were minutely and accurately measured. Unproductive effort was eliminated. Work activities were standardized for smooth and boosted production. Taylor's ideas were excellent but the dictatorial 'them and us' style of management generated ongoing resistance from successive labour forces.

Now, with an example from an oustandingly successful manufacturer in the USA the 'time and motion study' approach has gone full circle and is again in operation. But there is one significant difference: the stopwatches and the clipboards are in the hands of the workers, not the managers. New United Motor Manufacturing Inc. is a car factory in Fremont, California, jointly owned by General Motors and Toyota. Prior to the joint venture in 1983 the two rivals had very different approaches to management. The Fremont factory had a history of low productivity, wild-cat strikes, alcohol and drug abuse. Absenteeism was so high that hundreds of extra workers were employed just to ensure that enough people clocked in each day.

Initially the Toyota managers from Japan, seconded to run the new factory, proposed employing non-union labour. But General Motors feared sympathetic strike action from workers in their other factories and would not agree. When the new joint venture factory opened approximately 85 per cent of the 2,200 hourly workers came from the original workforce.

Two years later the production of the Fremont assembly line was higher than at any other General Motors factory, and more than twice as high as the level previously achieved at Fremont. Moreover, the earlier problems of alcoholism, drug abuse and absenteeism had virtually disappeared.

The Toyota managers had divided up the workforce into 350 teams of five to seven persons and a team leader. Every team was encouraged to analyse their own work performance through Taylor's time and motion study methods, striving to improve their performance. The team members designed all the teams' jobs. They then compared their efforts with those of other shifts doing the same kind of work. The process is continuous: teams strive always to get better. Team members were all trained to do each other's jobs and they regularly rotated their tasks and functions.

The Toyota/General Motors approach contrasts starkly with the earlier General Motors style of management. Before the merger, a team of industrial engineers roamed the factory designing jobs and work procedures and setting norms and standards. Without consultation the supervisors endeavoured to impose the procedures on the workforce. In Toyota/General Motors the worker's job has been drastically redesigned. But the function of the manager has not disappeared; there is no longer 'them and us' but the management function is as important as ever. Management supports the thinking workforce in whatever logistical or strategic ways necessary to help production grow. The difference between the 'before' and 'after' workforce is that the individual worker is encouraged to participate in decisions on the shop floor. Toyota achieved success in Fremont by persuading the workers that they were the key elements in the factory's success.

## The Place of Work

***Question: How important are physical working conditions?***

Few organizations set out to provide oppressive work surroundings. When conditions are bad it is because they have been allowed to deteriorate. Minimum criteria should be laid down, but if conditions are only borderline there is no question of any positive influence on employee relations. The main legislative Acts and Regulations relevant to working conditions are:

- Health and Safety at Work Act 1974.
- Offices Shops and Railway Premises Act 1963.
- Control of Substances Hazardous to Health Regulations 1988.
- Factories Act 1961.
- Fire Precautions Act 1971.
- First Aid Regulations 1982.
- Noise at Work Regulations 1982.
- Electricity at Work Regulations 1987.

The best way to ensure compliance with the legislation, and where possible to better it, is to have commitment from the top of the organization. For example, in respect of health and safety a Company Health and Safety Policy Statement can be issued and the employee or employees responsible for implementation identified. In addition, a responsibility statement should be given to all personnel setting out their obligations:

- Strict observance and implementation of the rules and systems set out in the health and safety policy and programme.
- Taking reasonable care for the individual's personal health and safety and that of fellow employees who are affected directly or indirectly by their actions.
- Reporting potential or actual hazards and defects promptly to the appropriate company officer.
- Taking part in the health and safety training programmes considered necessary by the company in order to comply with company health and safety policy and legislation.

- Being aware of the correct action to be taken in the event of accident, fire or other emergency.
- Cooperating with management and other personnel in meeting any statutory requirements.
- No interference with or misuse of anything provided to protect health, safety or welfare as required by legislation.

An understanding of the responsibilities within this statement by employees is important and should be confirmed as part of the employee induction programme.

Many companies form a joint consultative committee of management and employees to discuss and monitor health and safety issues. The issue of safety is underlined by the legal requirements, but in addition the perception of management caring about its workforce is important.

To ensure compliance with safety requirements all tasks carried out in the company should be assessed to determine the needs for safe working methods. Tasks involving risks must be documented and safe working methods enforced. Tasks that contain a high element of risk require the use of a written Permit to Work system.

The first step in establishing safe working methods is to carry out a job hazard analysis. Methodically, in turn, jobs are broken down into component tasks. Each task is then examined for any hazards. When hazards are identified, control measures should be developed to eliminate them or to reduce the risk of accident arising. The final step is to document safety instructions for the work procedure and ensure all relevant personnel are advised of the safety instructions.

Despite precautions, accidents in the workplace do occur. Whenever there is an accident it should be investigated by the line manager. If appropriate, specialist personnel — e.g. the safety officer or engineer — may be brought in to help decide on action to prevent any reoccurrence of that accident. For serious accidents the investigation is a statutory requirement. Accident investigations should be recorded on a standardized Accident Investigation Report form drawn up to incorporate all relevant details (see Figure 6.1).

For truly safe working conditions accurate accident statistics are essential. Figure 6.2 shows a simple form for use in analysing departmental and company accident absences. The Accident Injury Analysis shown in Figure 6.3 is particularly useful in identifying the three major elements of an accident: cause, site of injury and the nature of the injury. From these forms trends are discernable and the areas of potential danger highlighted.

| | | | | |
|---|---|---|---|---|
| 1. | Nature of accident: | | | |
| | Date: | Time: | Reported to: | Time: |
| | Exact location of accident: | | | |
| | Type of work: | | | |
| | Machine: | | | In motion: Yes/no |
| | Machine part causing injury: | | | |
| | Explain fully how accident occurred (with sketch plan if necessary): | | | |
| 2a. | Injured person:<br>Full name (Mr/Mrs/Miss):<br><br>Age: | Single/Married: | | |
| | Address: | | | |
| | Occupation: | | Length of service: | |
| | Total days away from work: | | From: | To: |
| | Nature and extent of injuries (i.e. part of body affected and type of injury: | | | |

| | |
|---|---|
| 2b. | Damage:<br>Nature and effect of damage (to property, plant or material) |
| 3. | Witnesses (or other persons interviewed):<br>Name (Mr/Mrs/Miss): Occupation/Position: |
| 4. | Causes of accident (Place a tick against each heading if it is considered to be one of the contributory factors to the accident):<br>(1) Design or layout of area (2) Construction of building<br>(3) Heat, light, ventilation (4) Operational method<br>(5) Mechanical or material failure (6) Machinery guards<br>(7) Maintenance (8) Need for protective equipment<br>(9) Design of protective equipment (10) Protective equipment not used<br>(11) Housekeeping (12) Supervision<br>(13) Training (14) Rules or instructions<br>(15) Breach of rules/instructions (16) Attitude to work<br>(17) Physical disability (18) Other (state) |
| 5. | Recommendations to prevent a recurrence:<br>What action is recommended to prevent another similar accident?<br><br>Date action taken: |
| 6, | Estimated cost of accident:<br>Property damage: £<br>Time lost by injured person: £<br>Product/material damage: £<br>Plant or machinery costs: £<br>Other costs: £<br>===========<br>TOTAL £ |
| | Accident investigated by: Date:<br><br>*Please use a separate sheet if necessary* |

*Figure 6.1. An accident investigation form.*

| Company: | | | Period from: | To: | | | |
|---|---|---|---|---|---|---|---|
| | Departments | | | | | | Total |
| | A | B | C | D | E | F | |
| Number of accidents | | | | | | | |
| From No. of accidents absence up to 3 days: | | | | | | | |
| From No. of accidents absence over 3 days: | | | | | | | |
| Total man-days absence 'X': | | | | | | | |
| Total man-days worked 'Y': | | | | | | | |
| % absence $\frac{X}{Y} \times 100$ | | | | | | | |

*Figure 6.2. Departmental accident absence record.*

| | Accidents per department | | | | | | Totals | | | |
|---|---|---|---|---|---|---|---|---|---|---|
| | A | B | C | D | E | F | Fatal | Major injury | Over 3 days | Other |
| *Cause of injury:* | | | | | | | | | | |
| Handling or lifting | | | | | | | | | | |
| Machinery | | | | | | | | | | |
| Person falling from height | | | | | | | | | | |
| Person falling on same level | | | | | | | | | | |
| Falling object | | | | | | | | | | |
| Stepping on/striking object | | | | | | | | | | |
| Hand tools | | | | | | | | | | |
| Other causes | | | | | | | | | | |
| Total | | | | | | | | | | |
| *Prime site of injury:* | | | | | | | | | | |
| Feet | | | | | | | | | | |
| Legs | | | | | | | | | | |
| Hands | | | | | | | | | | |
| Arms | | | | | | | | | | |
| Head and neck | | | | | | | | | | |
| Eyes | | | | | | | | | | |
| Trunk | | | | | | | | | | |
| Systemic | | | | | | | | | | |
| Total | | | | | | | | | | |
| *Prime nature of injury:* | | | | | | | | | | |
| Abrasions/skin wounds/ bruises | | | | | | | | | | |
| Foreign bodies/eye injuries | | | | | | | | | | |
| Crushing/concussion | | | | | | | | | | |
| Fracture dislocation | | | | | | | | | | |
| Amputation | | | | | | | | | | |
| Burn/scald | | | | | | | | | | |
| Strains/sprains/hernias | | | | | | | | | | |
| Gassing/poisoning/electric shock | | | | | | | | | | |
| Total | | | | | | | | | | |

*Figure 6.3. An accident injury analysis form.*

An important related aspect of accidents is cost. Accident costs are made up of:

- Loss of production resulting from the accident.
- Time spent in investigation.
- Remuneration paid to injured employee/employees whilst absent.
- Cost of additional labour to replace the injured employee or employees.
- The effect on insurance premiums.
- Damage to products, plant or machinery.

More difficult to quantify are the costs to the company in respect of the pain and suffering of an injured employee and the effect on work colleagues who have witnessed accidents.

A desirable precautionary measure is a periodic audit of the working environment to check safety standards. In high-risk environments the audit should be carried out on a daily basis; in other environments a weekly or monthly audit is appropriate. The audit should be carried out by a named individual — usually the line manager — or by a group of employees. An example of a safety checklist is given in Figure 6.4: this should be tailored to specific company locations and plant.

In addition to health and safety in the work environment there are three further aspects that must be addressed.

### *Temperature and humidity*

Extremes of temperature can play havoc with production. Factories and offices closed for the weekend at times when weather conditions are bad are cold and unwelcoming on Monday mornings. Similarly a contageous lethargy pervades all work when temperatures rise above 80 degrees with continuing hot weather. Management can reduce and even eliminate the transient temperature influences on production and on morale. The options are simple — air conditioning and supplementary heating — but there are costs. To balance against these costs is the added value benefit of employees' perception that management cares about working conditions.

### *Noise*

Noise, or the unusual absence of noise, is intrusive. An acceptable level of background noise is a form of security to a workforce. Optimum noise levels or desirable background music should be researched so that working conditions are best for the workforce.

In factories modification of equipment and the application of

| | Yes | No |
|---|---|---|
| *External*<br>1. Yard surface, roads, parking areas are in good repair | | |
| 2. Vehicular and pedestrian routes are adequately lighted | | |
| 3. Appropriate speed restrictions are enforced | | |
| *Structure and working environment*<br>4. Floors, stairs, walls and ceilings are in good condition | | |
| 5. All gantries and permanent and temporary openings in floors are securely fenced | | |
| 6. The area is free from tripping hazards (structural and removable) | | |
| 7. Vehicular and pedestrian routes are separated | | |
| 8. All lights are working | | |
| 9. The atmosphere is free from airborne dust, fumes and gases | | |
| 10. The temperature is comfortable (except in artificially controlled areas or storage areas) | | |
| *Machinery and equipment*<br>11. All dangerous parts of machines are guarded by either:<br>(i) securely fixed guards or machine casing<br>(ii) removable or hinged guards which are interlocked to the machine drive | | |
| *Electrical*<br>12. All flexes, cables, plugs and sockets are free from visible defects | | |
| 13. All flexes and leads to equipment are sited to avoid being run over or otherwise damaged | | |
| 14. Equipment can be isolated from the electricity supply by either:<br>(i) a switch capable of being locked off<br>(ii) removal of the plug from a socket | | |
| 15. All electrical hand tools are used at 110v | | |
| 16. Electrical panels are locked | | |
| *Fire*<br>17. All combustible material is stored away from heat sources | | |
| 18. Emergency exits are:<br>(i) clearly marked<br>(ii) unobstructed | | |
| 19. Fire extinguishers are readily accessible | | |
| 20. A fire alarm point is within easy reach of all employees working inside the building | | |

| | Yes | No |
|---|---|---|
| *Protective clothing and equipment* | | |
| 21. Ear defenders are worn in ear protection zones | | |
| 22. Respiratory protection is worn for designated tasks | | |
| 23. Other protective clothing/equipment is used where appropriate | | |
| 24. Issue is on a personal basis | | |
| *Housekeeping and cleaning* | | |
| 25. The workplace is clean, free from deposits of dust, accumulations of waste and spillages | | |
| 26. Passages and stairs are free from obstruction | | |
| 27. Materials are stored in a safe and tidy fashion | | |
| *Working practices* | | |
| 28. Persons working at heights are protected from falling | | |
| 29. Safety devices are free from interference | | |
| 30. Rider and pedestrian-operated trucks are used with care | | |
| 31. Ladders and other access equipment in use are sound and firmly secured | | |
| 32. Tools being used are in good condition | | |
| 33. Substances are correctly: (i) labelled (ii) stored (iii) used | | |
| 34. Stacked and palleted goods are stable and safe | | |
| 35. Reduction valves are fitted to compressed-air hoses | | |
| 36/ Operatives avoid using compressed air for blowing down: (i) machinery and structural surfaces (ii) themselves or their clothing | | |
| Completed by....................................... Date........... | | |

*Figure 6.4. A general health and safety checklist.*

acoustic materials can bring down unacceptable levels of noise. In open-plan offices, a rearrangement of work stations, with room dividers and filing cabinets positioned as a baffle, is helpful in creating privacy and reducing noise. When new equipment is purchased — whether a photocopier for the office or new equipment for the shop floor — the noise level emitted from the equipment has to be carefully considered.

### *Tools and equipment*

Many tools and much equipment are poorly designed. The problem is not exclusive to the workplace — it applies also to domestic equipment: for example, how many drivers can change stations on their car radio without taking their eyes off the road?

Poorly designed equipment affects performance. The problem may be that technology has overtaken events, and hand tools that were once effective are now limited in the functions they provide. A regular audit of tools and equipment from the point of view of the worker on the shop floor is recommended. But care is necessary: operatives adapt to their environment and generally are comfortable even with equipment that has become outdated. Evaluation of tools and equipment must not be interpreted by the workforce as a threat. The opinions of operatives using equipment on the shop floor must be taken into account in the evaluation process.

## A Contributory Factor

### *Question: How does well-designed communication enhance performance?*

Communication involves more than just words and pictures. Good communication embraces understanding. Jan Carlzon in his book *Moments of Truth* recounts an experience shortly after his appointment as President of Scandinavian Airlines. He was returning to Sweden from a visit to the USA. The baggage reclaim department was in turmoil. The monitors matching incoming flights to the allocated conveyer belts carrying passenger baggage were malfunctioning. Passengers did not know where to find their luggage. There was disorder and frustration.

Carlzon suggested to the employee at the information counter that a few signs be posted, handwritten if necessary, to help passengers retrieve their luggage. He was told that this suggestion had indeed been made to the person's manager a week ago, when the equipment had broken down. The reply had been that the equipment would be fixed promptly so there was no need for temporary signs. Carlzon remonstrated that now a week had passed. He was advised that the manager had again been told of the delay; his response was that since the delay had occurred the matter was sure to be dealt with right away.

As soon as Carlzon reached his office he telephoned the divisional manager. He offered a choice: either the manager moved his impressive desk from his large office and sited it in the arrivals terminal to see at first hand what was going on, or he could stay where he was — but in the second option he had to surrender decision-making power to those at the front line.

Technically there was no breakdown in communication between the person at the information counter and the manager concerned. Without any doubt there was immediate understanding that there was equipment malfunction. The full understanding of what was happening to the passengers was understood but ignored: they were only a few customers, and an airline has many. As the manager was physically remote from the situation it was not difficult to put out of mind. For good communication to be achieved, understanding between the communicating parties must have no limitations.

There is another issue that arises from this story. If front-line people are empowered to make decisions or to contribute to decision-making — and that is the philosophy of this book — what happens to the supervisors and managers? Are they to be redundant? Their skills and experience have valuable contributions to make but not necessarily in a traditional direct authoritative management style.

Communication between management and workforce must be two-way. Frequently it isn't. Often the workforce is ignorant of company progress, of how the specific jobs carried out by individuals relate to the overall scene. Management, to be effective, needs to know how the workforce perceives the company and how people see their jobs and their future.

Communication within an organization flows in three ways — downwards, upwards and laterally. In addition, there is the grapevine which spreads news of a football pool win or a departmental sacking instantaneously throughout the organization. Figure 6.5 illustrates the major channels in the communication process.

Channels grouped in the downwards communication flow encompass the different ways that management keeps company personnel informed. The more line management and the workforce know about the company direction and its successes, the more cohesive the company becomes. Opportunities to communicate range from one-to-one messages by means of letters or advisory meetings to the scattergun approach of the company noticeboard or house magazine.

Formal upward communication flow is derived from reports and meetings. Observation and personal contact provide other sources of information and equally tap communication data that is spreading horizontally through the organization.

Communication pathways in a company are frequently static. A drive towards enhanced employee performance usefully embraces an appraisal of communication flow and subsequent redesign. In many

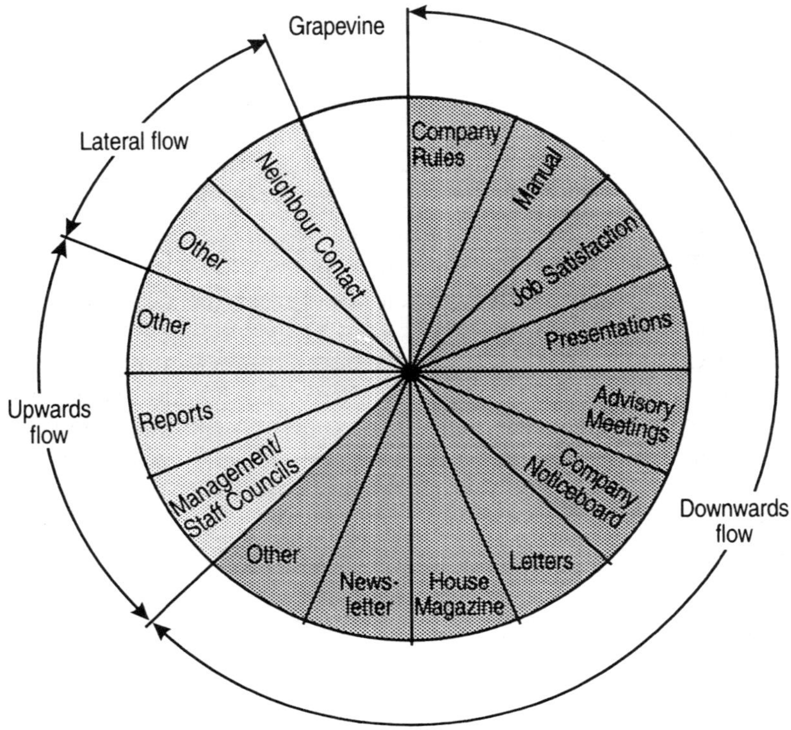


*Figure 6.5. The channels in the communication process.*

companies it is not uncommon to find that the workforce, the sales force and the service engineers have little contact with each other, and know relatively little about what the other employees really do. There may even be animosity because of differing rates of take-home pay.

Training sessions are recommended to which shop-floor supervisors, salesmen and service engineers should be invited. A warm-up exercise asks each person to describe 'a day in the working life of' the other two disciplines. The exercise is invariably revealing. The format of the training session generally is to discuss common problems and how they might be solved. Over and above any immediate practical solutions that are found, there is the enormous benefit of building closer links between members of the company. To cement the new positive relationships, a pretext must be found socially, or via inter-departmental competition, for regular contact.

## Summary

*Question:* What happens when design is poor?
*Answer:* Design in the workplace refers to the product, service, plant and layout, and to the job itself. All impinge on the behavioural aspects of the workforce. When design is poor there will be absenteeism, industrial accidents and product quality deficiencies.

*Question:* What are the ingredients of good job design?
*Answer:* Good job design is about humanizing jobs. A happy productive workforce needs clear goals, variety, responsibility, feedback, opportunities for self-development, resources to do the job, and involvement in decision-making for front-line matters.

*Question:* How important are physical working conditions?
*Answer:* Oppressive working conditions are counterproductive to sound employee relations. Health and safety factors, temperature, noise and the quality of tools and equipment have a direct influence on employee performance. There is legislation to cover minimum levels, but it is only the higher-quality levels that enhance performance.

*Question:* How does well-designed communication enhance performance?
*Answer:* Effective communication interfaces with good understanding and performance. Within a company there is a communication network with channels extending upwards, downwards and laterally. Management is recommended to appraise the network and reinforce it as necessary. The intended result is a cohesive workforce, participating in company progress.

# 7

# MANAGING EMPLOYEE RELATIONSHIPS

Before reading this chapter please answer the following questions. Each question is discussed in the text. At the end of the chapter questions and answers are collected together to form a summary.

## Questions

- Why should an employer recognize a trade union?
- In recognizing groups of workers, what aspects of recognition should management consider?
- How are collective procedures best described?
- What are the rights of trade union employee representatives?
- What are the ramifications of consultative arrangements?
- What problems must be overcome in implementing employee consultative programmes?

## Establishing Identity
### *Question: Why should an employer recognize a trade union?*

The wishes of employees and potential employees in a company are, of necessity, a very important consideration. Many employees, because of their experience, traditions, and a prevailing attitude towards work, expect a 'recognition agreement' with their employer. This recognition agreement is a cornerstone of modern industrial relations. It is an agreement whereby an employer recognizes a union to represent a group of workers for the purpose of collective bargaining.

In industry today it is often the norm for organizations to depend on the consent of employees to manage effectively. It has not always been like this. In the short term, pressure can be applied to force consent from the employees, but in the long term, sustained and productive consent has to be earned, and it is earned by management paying attention to employee relationships.

Many new employers choose to have a recognition agreement from Day 1, as well as agreeing the choice of union. Examples are the many Japanese companies who have set up in the United Kingdom and have recognition agreements with a single union. From the employer's point of view there are positive benefits in the existence of a representative with whom to discuss common problems. An excellent channel of communication is established in this way.

Within employee relationships there are two main areas: collective agreements and consultative arrangements. Both play a vital role in maintaining and improving employee relationships. When the experience of employees within their employment is not good it encourages them to join a trade union and seek recognition: invariably this is the result of poor management. In greenfield sites where employees elect to have a recognition agreement and choose a single union, they avoid the problems associated with multi-unions. For existing employees without a collective agreement, but with trade union membership, the problem arises for the employer of when to recognize a union, and in what manner. If recognition is given to too few union members, other employees may become disenchanted. A union with a small membership is also likely to create a clique, antagonizing other workers in the process.

Where union membership is very high, and the employer refuses recognition, the employer risks antagonizing the majority of the workforce. The inevitable end is some form of industrial action.

A major concern of employers is that without a recognition agreement, employees can choose to join different trade unions. The employer can then be forced to recognize a number of different unions, representing different groups of workers.

When an employer reaches the decision that a recognition agreement with a particular union is in its best interests, a ballot should be promptly arranged. This ballot will focus simply on recognition with employees, who still have the option to join or not join a union. In voting to recognize a particular trade union, employees are under no obligation to join that trade union. A simple majority in favour of recognition is sufficient for recognition rights to be granted.

When support is gained from the workforce for recognition, an employer then needs to discuss and reach agreement with the union on the basis of recognition. The range of topics forming the basis of recognition includes anything that might be contained in a contract of employment between the employer and the groups of employees represented by a union or unions.

Separate groups of employees can cause difficulties for management. The exclusion of any group from the recognition agreement allows them the opportunity to join another union and seek recognition. If the group is too large, its members may not have enough common interests for representation to be feasible. If the group is too small, there may be other employees outside of the group who claim the same treatment because their terms and conditions of employment are similar. If the employer concedes the same benefits it can upset the union, which may argue that non-union employees are benefiting from their representation. If the employer refuses, it upsets the claimants.

In his early career, one of the authors worked with an engineering company in the North of England. In his capacity as personnel manager, he reached agreement with the union representing manual workers on a pay claim. But the agreement was only reached after industrial action had taken place, with non-union members working normally. In the negotiations the union insisted that the pay award should be paid only to union members. It was adamant that non-union members were to receive no increase. The argument, in justification, was that union members through industrial action had won improved terms and conditions — and by withholding a pay increase to non-union members it would encourage union membership.

The company refused to agree on the basis that employees on the same grade should receive the same pay. The union's response was to call a one-day stoppage in protest at the decision. After protracted and difficult negotiations it was finally agreed that all employees would receive the pay award, but that non-union members were to be encouraged to join the trade union. The encouragement was to be through a joint approach by management and union.

Following such action, union membership increased from 65 per cent to 85 per cent by the time of the following year's negotiations. No further problems arose in respect of union and non-union members.

## Who Does What

***Question: In recognizing groups of workers, what aspects of recognition should management consider?***

Within the total workforce there is a major boundary between manual and white-collar workers. But there are other sub-boundaries, too: for manual workers there are skills boundaries; within white-collar workers there are boundaries between supervisory, technical, clerical and administrative areas.

When these groups are identified, agreement should be reached with the trade union on how the groups are to be represented. The Amalgamated Engineering and Electrical Union, for example, represents employees who are skilled, semi-skilled and unskilled, but the membership grades are different and the arrangement with the employer recognizes such differences. The union, through its technical and supervisory section, represents white-collar employees with different officials and agreements. Other unions have similar arrangements.

For the employer, recognition of a trade union coupled with identification of discrete groups of employees represents the beginning of positive change. From that time onwards notice must be taken of what union representatives say and their point of view must be accommodated, even when there are collective procedures to be agreed.

## A Definition

***Question: How are collective procedures best described?***

Collective procedures provide a structure within which management and union representatives engage each other in discussion to resolve problems. This provides an opportunity to negotiate terms and conditions of employment. The procedures predetermine how matters are to be handled, so that everyone knows the next step if a problem is not resolved or agreement not reached. It is common practice for there to be three sections:

- General principles of recognition.

- Procedures to cover discipline (See Chapter 8).
- Procedures to cover grievance.

An example of a collective agreement is given on page 131, together with an example of Shop Stewards Credentials and Disciplinary Procedure and Rules, all as agreed between RHM Ingredients Ltd and the Union of Shop, Distributive and Allied Workers.

## Permitted Activities

***Question: What are the rights of trade union employee representatives?***

When a trade union gains recognition, the number of trade union representatives will be agreed. To maintain good working relationships, it is necessary to ensure that those employees elected as representatives are provided with the necessary skills to carry out their duties. The law gives the right to union representatives to paid time off for training, provided that the training is approved by the Trade Union Council (TUC) or the representative's own union.

Once a trade union has been recognized, the law also provides a statutory right for representatives to take off a reasonable amount of time from work for purposes connected with the conduct of workplace industrial relations. Paid time off is allowed to carry out union duties. Unpaid time off is permitted to take part in other union activities.

Typically, trade union duties are:

- Collective bargaining with company management.
- Informing members about negotiations.
- Consultations with management.
- Meeting with other union representatives or full-time officers on industrial matters concerning the union and the employer.
- Attending interviews with and on behalf of employees on grievance and disciplinary matters.
- Appearing on behalf of employees before an outside body — e.g. an industrial tribunal.
- Explaining to a new employee the role of the union in the workplace.

Trade union activities include:

- Taking part in meetings of union policy-making bodies.
- Attending the union annual conference.

- Representing the union on external bodies.
- Voting in union elections.

It is for the company and the trade union to agree what is reasonable time off. This varies from company to company depending upon the operational requirements and service to the company's customers. Representatives seeking time off must ensure that management is informed, as far in advance as is practical, indicating the nature of the business, the location and the anticipated period of absence. Management and trade unions will agree, when necessary, for other employees to cover the work of representatives absent on union business.

At all stages of collective bargaining there is a legal requirement on the employer to disclose any information requested by representatives of trade unions necessary to assist them in their negotiations.

However, an employer is not obliged to disclose information if:

- It is likely to cause substantial injury to the undertaking.
- It is against the interest of national security.
- It contravenes a prohibition order.
- It is given in confidence to an employer.
- It relates to an individual, without the individual's prior consent.

Information requested by trade unions relates generally to:

- Remuneration.
- Conditions of service.
- Manpower requirements.
- Performance indicators.

Management and trade unions should seek agreement on how the provisions on disclosure of information are to be implemented. This agreement should set out what is to be available, how it is to be presented, when it will be presented, and to whom.

Union recognition, collective agreements and the effect of the Employer Protection Act 1975 on these arrangements can make life difficult for employers. It is especially difficult for employers without specialist personnel staff. The Advisory, Conciliation and Arbitration Service (ACAS) provides a free service to any employer wishing advice in these areas. ACAS addresses are listed at the end of this chapter.

## A Positive Function

### *Question: What are the ramifications of consultative arrangements?*

Employee consultation is a process of employee involvement designed to provide employees with an opportunity of influencing proposals before a final decision is made. For the employer, consultation seeks to improve the efficiency and effectiveness of the organization by making sure that the decision-making is with the understanding and, where practical, the acceptance of employees. The principles embodied in an employee consultative programme involve:

- A requirement of a high degree of common interest and mutual interdependence between employer, employees, shareholders and the customer.
- All employees should be covered by consultative arrangements, from the shop floor upwards. Opportunities should be created for involving employees in areas relevant to their work interests, where the employee's skills and experience can contribute to meeting the company's objectives.
- The full involvement of representatives of trade unions recognized by management.
- The focus of all consultative arrangements should be on increasing the profitability and success of the organization, by increasing the sense of common purpose and by the motivation of all employees to maximize their contributions to the organization's success.
- The introduction of employee consultative arrangements places demands on management time and performance. Appropriate training to meet such demands must be provided to maximize the contribution to the consultative process.

There is no single uniform approach to the design of a consultative programme: organizations are too varied for such a simplistic solution. However, there are a number of basic guidelines that can assist management in formulating an employee consultative programme:

- Consultative programmes should be distinct from collective bargaining arrangements.
- Consultation requires behaviour that is supportive and conducive to discussion. This is in contrast to the inherent conflict of collective bargaining and negotiation.
- Consultation must cover all employees, incorporating all groups at all levels. It should strive towards the integration of union and

non-union employees.

- To be worthwhile consultative programmes must be integrated into the management decision-making process.
- It is essential to recognize that accountability for decision-making rests with management.
- Agenda items should reflect those issues and events of direct interest and concern to employees.

## Dealing with Difficulties

***Question: What problems must be overcome in implementing employee consultative programmes?***

Trade unions often insist that participation in any arrangements is restricted solely to trade union members. This can be a point of conflict for some companies with trade union representation. Consultative programmes are intended to cover all employees but circumstances occur where there are a number of different unions, with different membership levels, who negotiate separately and refuse to cooperate in consultative arrangements. Inter-union rivalry on occasion creates considerable problems that are very difficult to resolve.

Where trade union attitudes cannot be overcome, management has to consider seriously the value of any consultative arrangements that do not cover all employees. Groups excluded from consultative arrangements easily become disillusioned and demotivated. Progress on the introduction and development of consultative arıangements can only be made at the pace with which management can obtain the commitment and willingness of employee groups to look beyond their sectional interests, to the needs of the organization as a whole.

Another problem that can arise is in the relationship between employee consultation and collective bargaining. In any agreement on consultation, there is a need to state quite clearly that the purpose of the meeting is to be advisory and consultative. Very often matters that start off in the consultative process end up unintentionally in the negotiative process. Unfortunately this occurs quite easily, particularly when consultative forums consist solely of union representatives. Management put a proposal on the table for consultation: the representatives suggest amendments to the original proposal; management do not make clear that these counter proposals are unacceptable, neither as a whole nor in part.

At a later date management implement the proposals. The representatives then claim that at a previous meeting objections and counter proposals were submitted, which they believed were accepted by management, because no specific rejections were made by management at that time. The normal management reaction to this is that as no formal acceptance of the counter proposals was made, no binding agreement was reached.

An example of the confusion that can occur is as follows. Management propose that the company can no longer afford to subsidize the cost of food provided in the company canteen. Prices are to rise on average by 15 per cent. The representatives are unhappy with the proposal and suggest that prices should not increase to a level greater that the cost of living increase negotiated with the union. Management agree to consider the suggestion. One month later a pay increase of 8 per cent is agreed with the union. Two months later, management introduce a revised catering price list with increases averaging 15 per cent.

Three months later at the next consultative meeting, the representatives object to the price increase. They claim that as management had agreed to consider their counter proposal and as no objections had been received they believed that the counter proposals had been accepted. Management's response is that they only agreed to consider the proposal. Representatives argue that no agreement was reached on the canteen prices.

For this and other reasons many trade unions oppose the consultative process. They prefer management to make a decision, with collective bargaining then opposing or modifying the decision, when appropriate.

The tendency for consultation to develop into negotiation is another reason for having all employees represented on consultative committees. If representatives are not in a position to negotiate on behalf of their constituents, then no negotiation can take place: an exchange of views is not seen as negotiation.

The problem of negotiation can be overcome by specifying the topics to be discussed: any topics that are subject to negotiation are eliminated. However, this can lead to trivialities being discussed, with the real issues covered by the collective negotiation process.

Another problem may be a gradual unwitting change in the credibility of the representative. There is a reason for this: training is given to the representative to understand and interpret the range of information with which he or she is presented when carrying out official duties. Because of the training, a gap develops between the representative's perception of a situation and the perception of the others involved. One example was a company that increased its profits, year on year, but whose return on capital decreased. The representative saw this situation as a decrease in company performance: the others as an increase in performance. Generally, managers take a different view of matters because they are better informed and because of their trained ability to interpret information.

Given the same information and understanding it is likely that other representatives will reach the same conclusions as the manager. Constant contact with management results in some 'management thinking' rubbing off. As a result, the representative can be seen to be management orientated — the word 'tainted' is sometimes used. Once this perception develops, credibility is lost. The representative is not re-elected, and management is faced with an additional training requirement, and perhaps disruption to an effective consultative forum.

The complexities of companies determine that the format of consultative committees varies enormously; there is no off-the-shelf format that applies to any one company, but the example of the constitution of a consultative council given on page 139 covers all the salient points required.

---

## Recognition and Procedural Agreement between RHM Ingredients Ltd and Union of Shop, Distributive and Allied Workers

1.00 **Introduction**

1.1. This Agreement has been reached between RHM Ingredients and the Union of Shop, Distributive and Allied Workers in order to provide a system of representation and a procedure through which the parties will raise and discuss issues of common concern.

1.2 Both parties will recognise the the value of :-

(a) A working relationship between Management and employees based on mutual understanding and respect whereby questions which may arise affecting all employees or a body of employees, or individuals, can be promptly discussed through the medium of the Management and Trade Union structure.

b) Good communication through the medium of the Management and Trade Union structure.

c) The avoidance of disputes and the settlement of issues at the earliest possible opportunity and according to the agreed procedures.

2.0 **General Principles**

2.1 The Company recognises the Union of Shop, Distributive and Allied Workers as the sole body to represent and negotiate on behalf of employees covered by the Agreement.

2.2 The Union recognises the right of the Company to manage its affairs while the Company accepts that the Union can negotiate terms and conditions of employment on behalf of its members, in accordance with this Agreement.

2.3 Both parties have a common objective to use the process of negotiation to achieve mutually acceptable results. To this end they agree not to cause any undue delay in operating the procedure set forth in the Agreement and no stoppage of work or other restrictions or coercive action of any kind on any disputed issues will take place until the procedure has been followed through to its conclusion. The Company will similarly not lock out employees without recourse to the procedures agreed.

2.4 While the parties have every intention of honouring both the letter and the spirit of the Agreement, it is not intended to constitute a legally enforceable Agreement between the parties.

2.5 The Management will recognise a Union structure consisting of a Senior Union Representative plus three shift representatives elected from amongst the Union Members, in accordance with the Union rules and accredited in writing by the Union. Employees standing for the position of shop steward should have a minimum of 12 months' continuous service with the Company at the date of election.

2.6 The Management shall recognise Safety Representatives (in accordance with Health and Safety at Work, etc., Act 1974 and any subsequent legislation), who have been duly elected from amongst Union Members and accredited by the Union. Those recognised will participate in the Health and Safety committee in accordance with the RHM Health and Safety policy.

2.7 In order to ensure that fair and effective arrangements exist for dealing with disciplinary matters, the Management and the Union have agreed on a disciplinary procedure as set out in the standard terms and conditions of employment.

2.8 The Company is firmly committed to pursuing a policy of equality of opportunity and there is no differentiation in the terms and conditions of employment or treatment of employees on the basis of sex, marital status, creed, colour, race or ethnic origin. Relevant information will be made available, on request, to the Trade Union to confirm the operation of this policy.

2.9 The employees are committed to give a maximum cooperation to do their utmost to maintain and increase production, to give their full cooperation in efforts to reduce waste of materials power, etc., and to give reasonable assistance to the Company in the application of scientific methods and labour-saving machinery as may be considered necessary, so that in order to meet competition the fullest possible output may be secured. The Company in its turn agrees that it shall not implement any changes to existing work practices until agreement has been reached or the negotiating procedure exhausted.

---

**Shop Steward's Credentials**

1. He/she will be recognised as an accredited representative for two years from the date of election. If he/she ceases to be an employee of the Company, or a member of the Union, his/her appointment as a representative automatically ceases.

2. When acting in his/her Union capacity, he/she shall be subject to the rules and regulations of the Union.

3. He/she agrees to abide, and to use his/her best endeavours to see that members abide, by all present and future agreements (of which he/she will receive copies) between the Company and the Union.

4. He/she will continue to be a working member of his/her department, but with the permission of his/her manager, which will not be unreasonably withheld, he/she may leave his/her work to

conduct Union business and may have access to any member(s) whom he/she represents. When visiting other departments, Union representatives will contact appropriate management seeing members on Union business.

5. His/her average earnings will be maintained where time off is taken during normal working hours, in pursuit of trade union activities, for which he/she is a member, and where he/she is acting as a representative of the Union, in connection with employment with RHM Ingredients, excluding activities which constitute industrial action.

6. Action taken by him/her in good faith in pursuance of his/her duties shall in no way affect his/her employment with the Company.

7(a) He/she will be granted reasonable facilities in order to assist him/her in the efficient completion of his/her duties, which will include access to a telephone, copying facilities, designated union noticeboards, office services and training. (Production requirements of the Company may reduce the availability of employees for training during certain periods.)

7(b) Display of official TU notices by official TU representatives on TU noticeboards will not require management approval.

8. The number of shop stewards needed and the departments they represent will be mutually determined between the Company and the Union.

9. Disciplinary interviews or action will only take place in respect of the shop steward or deputy shop steward with the involvement of the Area Official.

10. In order to promote an atmosphere conducive to good industrial relations the Shop Steward will be fully involved in the induction of new employees and specific time will be allocated to enable the explanation of agreements, Union rules and benefits.

## Disciplinary Procedure and Rules

### 1.0 Introduction

The Company expects the highest standards of discipline in all its departments and believes that to preserve this standard and to safeguard the interests of both the Company and its employees, there should be a well defined disciplinary procedure which is properly understood by everyone and which will ensure a uniform approach. All members of management are responsible for ensuring that Company rules and standards are understood and maintained. All employees should familiarise themselves with this procedure and with Company rules and standards of conduct.

### 2.0 Aim of Disciplinary Procedure

The aim of the disciplinary procedure is corrective and not punitive. It is designed to discourage further breaches of discipline and encourage improved standards of conduct.

### 3.0 Procedure

At all stages of this procedure employees will be given the opportunity to prepare their case when they are being subjected to disciplinary action.

3.1 Stage 1 — Misconduct (see Disciplinary Rules)

In the case of proven misconduct, a formal verbal warning will be given and will constitute the first stage of the disciplinary procedure. This formal verbal warning will normally be given by that employee's manager, who will inform the employee that the warning given will constitute the first formal stage of the disciplinary procedure. The date and reason for issue of a verbal warning will be recorded on a Disciplinary Action Form (see Appendix) and be kept on file for a period of three months. The employee's union representative will be present, unless the individual concerned waives this right.

3.2 Stage 2 — Repeated Misconduct

In the case of repeated misconduct following a formal verbal warning, the employee will be interviewed by his/her manager. At this interview the employee will be given the opportunity to hear the complaint against him/her and state his/her case. If after full examination of the facts and circumstances of the case a written warning is justified, the employee will be told this by the departmental manager, who will issue the employee with a Disciplinary Action Form stating the nature of the misconduct. This written warning will remain on file for a period of six months. The employee's union representative will be present unless the individual concerned waives the right.

3.3 Stage 3 — Serious Misconduct or Related Misconduct Following Stages 1 and 2

This stage will apply when previous verbal and written warnings have failed to improve or rectify the situation or where serious misconduct has occurred. The employee concerned will be interviewed by his departmental manager and will have the opportunity of stating his/her case. If after full examination of the facts and circumstances of the case a final written warning is justified, the employee will be told by his/her departmental manager who will confirm the matter in writing using a Disciplinary Action Form. In cases of serious misconduct it may be appropriate, depending upon the circumstances, to suspend the employee without pay for a maximum of three days. A final written warning will remain on file for a period of twelve months. The employee's union representative will be present, unless the individual concerned waives this right.

3.4 Stage 4 — Gross Misconduct, Repeated Serious Misconduct or Misconduct following Stages 1, 2 and 3

This stage will apply when Stages 1, 2 and 3 have failed to improve or rectify the situation or where a gross misconduct has occurred. The employee concerned will be interviewed by the Senior Site Manager and the Departmental Manager concerned and will have the opportunity of stating his/her case. If, after a full examination of the facts and circumstances of the case, disciplinary action is warranted, this will normally be dismissal without notice in the case of gross misconduct or repeated misconduct. Depending upon the merits of the case it may be considered appropriate as an alternative to dismissal to suspend the employee without pay up to a maximum of five days, and/or demotion in the case of someone in a post of responsibility. In the case of dismissal, this will be confirmed in writing and will state the reasons for the decision and the right of appeal. The employee's union representative will be present, unless the employee requests otherwise in writing, waiving his/her rights to union representation.

3.5 Appeal Procedure

If an employee decides to appeal against disciplinary action the disputes/grievance procedure will apply — commencing at the level of management above that involved in taking the decision relating to Disciplinary Action.

3.6 Suspension During Investigation

The Company may decide to suspend any employee with no loss of pay in any case of alleged misconduct in order that a full and thorough investigation of the facts of the case can be made. This suspension will in no way prejudice the outcome of the investigation or any resultant disciplinary action.

3.7 Records

The records of formal disciplinary warnings, disciplinary suspension and demotions will lapse after three months. All first written warnings will be recorded in the employee's personal file for a period of six months. Final written warnings will remain on file for a period of twelve months. Details of all disciplinary action will be given to the Senior Union Representative. Warnings that have not expired will be taken into consideration when considering further misconduct.

4.0 **Disputes/Grievance Procedure**

4.1 This procedure has been designed to provide a clearly understood means of resolving disputes/grievances as quickly as possible and at the lowest possible level. Whilst matters are being dealt with under this procedure, there shall be no lock-out, strikes, overtime ban or any other interference with normal practices and the general principle of status quo will be observed.

4.2 Application of the Procedure

Matters arising will be dealt with under a four-stage procedure. The detailed application with levels of Management and Union Representative involved is described in the Appendix to this Agreement. In general terms the stages will operate as follows:

*Stage 1.* Individual, Union Representative and Departmental Management.
*Stage 2.* Union Representative/Production Manager.
*Stage 3.* Union Official (Area Officer)/Factory Manager Personnel Manager.
*Stage 4.* Union Official (Area Officer/Divisional Officer) Operations Director, Personnel Manager.

At each stage a Procedure Report Form will be completed (see Appendix). If the issue raised affects employees in a number of different departments the procedure may start at Stage 2. Negotiation on changes to general conditions such as pay, holidays, etc., which normally take place annually will be dealt with initially at Stage 2.

**General**

1.0 This Agreement shall be terminated only upon three months' notice, in writing, given by either party to the other.

2.0 Whilst both parties to the Agreement consider it binding in honour upon them, it is agreed that it is not legally enforceable.

3.0 This Agreement shall take effect from.............

Signed for and on behalf of RHM INGREDIENTS LIMITED

............................................................

Signed for and on behalf of U S D A W

............................................................ Dated................................

## XYZ Company Consultative Council

### Constitution

1. **Name**

The Council shall be called the XYZ Consultative Committee.

2. **Purpose**

The purpose of the Council shall be to provide a means of regular consultation between management and representatives of employees. It shall cover all matters of mutual interest other than those matters which are negotiated by the trade unions.

3. **Membership**

The Council shall consist of nine elected members, and three members including the Chairman will be appointed by the Company.

3.1 For membership of the Council an employee who has been employed by the Company for not less than two years shall be eligible for nomination and election to the Council.

3.2 The following departments shall each have elected representatives on the Council as shown:

| | |
|---|---|
| Production | 2 |
| Distribution | 1 |
| Engineering | 1 |
| Sales and Marketing | 1 |
| Technical | 1 |
| Finance | 1 |
| Personnel | 1 |

3.3 The Council shall have the authority to co-opt any employee as a temporary non-voting member for discussion on a specific subject.

4. **Officers**

The Chairman of the Council will be appointed by the

Company. The Vice Chairman will be chosen from the Council and will be elected by Council members for a term of two years after which the member may be re-elected.

5. **Service**

5.1 One third of the elected representatives shall retire each year in rotation but may offer themselves for re-election.

5.2 Should a member leave the Company or resign from the Council the vacancy shall be filled by a by-election in the same way as for annual elections. The newly elected member will take over the remaining term of office of the member leaving.

6. **Elections**

6.1 These shall take place in March each year and the members elected will take up appointment from April 1st. The Council shall appoint a Returning Officer who will make all necessary arrangements for holding elections.

6.2 Notice of elections. At least four weeks before the date of the election, notice of election will be posted stating:

Date of election
Last date for receipt of nominations
Details of voting departments
Name of Returning Officer
Any other relevant information

6.3 Procedure for nomination. After posting of notice of election, nomination forms will be available from the Returning Officer. Completed nomination forms showing names of candidates, proposer and seconder should be delivered to the Returning Officer within two weeks of the date of the election.

6.4 Procedure for election. Having confirmed that nominees are willing to stand at least one week prior to polling date the Returning Officer will post notice of nominations.

7. **Meetings**

The Council shall meet on the 2nd Wednesday of each month

excluding December and August. Special meetings may be called by Chairman or at the request of the majority of the members. Items for the agenda shall be notified to the secretary by the first Wednesday of each month and the agenda issued to members three days prior to date of meeting.

8. **Quorum**

Two thirds of members shall form a quorum.

9. **Minutes**

Minutes shall be made of all meetings and, after confirmation by the Chairman or Vice Chairman, shall be circulated to all members as soon as possible after a meeting. Minutes shall also be displayed on departmental noticeboards.

10. **Alterations of Constitution**

Any alteration to the constitution shall require a 75 per cent vote in favour of the motion by the whole Council and the approval of the Company Directors.

## ACAS addresses

*Northern Region*

Westgate House, Westgate Road, Newcastle upon Tyne NE1 1TJ
Tel: Newcastle upon Tyne (091) 261 2191 Fax: (091) 232 5452

| | | |
|---|---|---|
| Cumbria | Tyne and Wear | Cleveland |
| Northumberland | Durham | |

*Yorkshire and Humberside Region*

Commerce House, St Albans Place, Leeds LS2 8HH
Tel: Leeds (0532) 431371 Fax: (0532) 446678

| | | |
|---|---|---|
| North Yorkshire | South Yorkshire | Humberside |
| West Yorkshire | | |

*London Region*

Clifton House, 83-117 Euston Road, London NW1 2RB
Tel: 071-388 5100 Fax: 071-388 9722

*South East Region*

Westminster House, Fleet Road, Fleet, Hants, GU13 8PD
Tel: Fleet (0252) 811868 Fax: (0252) 617006

| | | |
|---|---|---|
| Cambridgeshire | Hertfordshire | Hampshire (except Ringwood) |
| Norfolk | Essex | |
| Suffolk | Berkshire | Isle of Wight |
| Oxfordshire | Surrey | East Sussex |
| Buckinghamshire | Kent | West Sussex |
| Bedfordshire | | |

*South West Region*

Regent House, 27a Regent Street, Clifton, Bristol BS8 4HR
Tel: Bristol (0272) 744066 Fax: (0272) 744078

| | | |
|---|---|---|
| Gloucestershire | Cornwall | Dorset |
| Avon | Devon | Ringwood |
| Wiltshire | Somerset | |

*Midlands Region*

Leonard House, 319/323 Bradford Street, Birmingham B5 6ET
Tel: Birmingham (021) 622 5050 Fax: (021) 622 2244

| | | |
|---|---|---|
| Staffordshire | Hereford and Worcester | |
| Shropshire | West Midlands | Warwickshire |

*Nottingham Office:* Anderson House, Clinton Avenue, Nottingham NG5 1AW Tel: Nottingham (0602) 693355 Fax: (0602) 693085

| | | |
|---|---|---|
| Derbyshire (except High Peak District) | Leicestershire<br>Northamptonshire | Lincolnshire<br>Nottinghamshire |

*North West Region*

Boulton House, 17-21 Chorlton Street, Manchester Ml 3HY
Tel: Manchester (061) 228 3222 Fax: (061) 228 7975

| | | |
|---|---|---|
| Cheshire | Greater Manchester | High Peak District of Derbyshire |

*Merseyside Office:* Cressington House, 249 St Mary's Road, Garston, Liverpool L19 0NF
Tel: Liverpool (051) 427 8881 Fax: (051) 427 2715

*Lancashire Office:* Bradshawgate House, 1 Oak Street, Accrington, Lancs BB5 1EQ
Tel: Accrington (0254) 871996 Fax: (0254) 383348

*Scotland*

Franborough House, 123-157 Bothwell Street, Glasgow G2 7JR
Tel: Glasgow (041) 204 2677 Fax: (041) 221 4697

*Wales*

Phase 1, Ty Glas Road, Llanishen, Cardiff CF4 5PH
Tel: Cardiff (0222) 762636 Fax: (0222) 751334

*Head Office*

27 Wilton Street, London SW1X 7AZ
Tel: 071-210 3000 Fax: 071-210 3708

---

## Summary

*Question:* Why should an employer recognize a trade union?

*Answer:* A recognition agreement is such that an employer recognizes a union to represent a group of workers for the purposes of collective bargaining. It is a foundation stone of modern industrial relations.

*Question:* In recognizing groups of workers, what aspects of recognition should management consider?

*Answer:* A significant aspect of recognition is grouping of workers by skills and occupation. A major division is between manual and white-collar workers. Within the groups of white-collar workers boundaries exist between supervisory, technical and clerical and administrative functions. Manual workers are distinguished by their trades.

*Question:* How are collective procedures best described?
*Answer:* Collective procedures are a predetermined process established for management and union representatives to meet and resolve problems through discussion and negotiation. Because the procedures are established, the sequence of the steps is known to both parties.

*Question:* What are the rights of trade union employee representatives?
*Answer:* By statute, representatives of trade unions recognized by management are entitled to paid time off for training and union duties, with unpaid time off to take part in union activities. Trade union duties and activities are clearly defined and agreed.

*Question:* What are the ramifications of consultative arrangements?
*Answer:* A consultative arrangement is a recognized process of employee involvement and discussion with management. The objective is to provide employees with an opportunity of influencing management decision-making. Guidelines exist to help different companies with their unique problems formulate employee consultative programmes.

*Question:* What problems must be overcome in implementing employee consultative programmes?
*Answer:* Trade unions frequently attempt to restrict consultative programmes solely to trade union members, although such programmes are intended to cover all employees. This is a problem. Further troubles arise from inter-union conflict where there are different unions, with different membership levels, some of whom insist on negotiating separately. Another problem arises from programmes intended as employee consultations turning into collective bargaining. For this reason some unions oppose the consultative process. On occasion a problem may arise in the diminishing credibility of the union representative. Specific training

for union duties and increased involvement in management-type problems unwittingly distances the representative from his or her former colleagues. When the representative fails to gain re-election management is faced with fresh training and disruption.

# 8

# MONITORING EMPLOYEE PERFORMANCE

As with the other chapters you are invited to answer the following questions before reading the text. At the end of the chapter questions and answers appear together as a summary.

## Questions

- What are the major systems of appraisal used to monitor employee performance?
- What are the practical stages to an appraisal interview?
- What are the contributory factors to poor performance?
- How does the counselling interview help to resolve the problems of poor performance?
- What are the parameters of disciplinary procedure?
- What are the stages of disciplinary action?
- What are the ingredients of good discipline management?

## Making Regular Checks

### *Question: What are the major systems of appraisal used to monitor employee performance?*

The appraisal process is a valuable tool. The appraisal interview itself serves a number of purposes:

- To gather information and evidence.
- To remove uncertainties that exist and strengthen understanding.
- To agree a plan of future action.
- To motivate employees through encouragement and praise.
- To improve performance.

Clearly, to make progress companies need a method of appraising employees that really works. There are two major traditional systems:

- *Performance review.* This is linked with performance improvement. The aim is to improve corporate organizational performance by improving the performance of individual employees.
- *Review of employee potential.* The potential of individual employees is assessed as to the capability for development beyond the limitations of their present scale of work.

### *Performance review*

Performance review is the most frequently used system. To implement appraisal there are two methods of approach:

*1. The objectives scheme.* Here managers and employees work to achieve objectives and standards of performance that are to be met within a set period. Usually this scheme applies to white-collar workers. The timescale of appraisal is generally one year, but as long as the logistics of conducting appraisal interviews do not get in the way, it is advantageous to make the appraisal meetings more frequent — every six months is good; every three months is better. When there is a positive relationship between manager and employee, feedback on good performance is a great motivator.

The divisional, departmental or sectional objectives that are set are themselves directed at achieving part of the overall corporate objectives. In current business practice the setting of aims and objectives is often confused — the two meanings are interchanged or mixed up with strategies and tactics. An *aim* is where the company or person wants to go — it is sometimes called a 'mission statement'. An *objective* is what the company or person has to do to get there.

| Job holder: Factory manager | Performance objectives for review period:............................ | |
|---|---|---|
| Key objectives in order of priority | Measures and standards of performance required | Evaluation of performance against objectives (note any change in circumstances which affected original objective) |
| 1. Quality BS 5750 | To achieve BS 5750 accreditation by end June | |
| 2. Customer complaints | To reduce customer complaints by 10% in 1994 on 1993 figures. | |
| 3. Absence levels | By end of 1994 to reduce absence levels to 3.5% | |
| 4. Capital equipment | To prepare capital authority requisition for new packing machine by April | |
| 5. Communication | To carry out audit into company communication and produce report for September management meeting | |

*Figure 8.1. Performance review objectives.*

Objectives must be realistic. They must be achievable but at the same time they should stretch the individual. If the objectives are beyond reach there will be demotivation. Equally important is that the objectives are precise and quantifiable, and relate to a set period of time. If performance cannot be measured, how can it be evaluated effectively? A practical rule is that ten objectives is the maximum number to be set for any employee.

Figure 8.1 illustrates a typical set of performance review objectives. At the end of the review period a performance review meeting is held between the boss and subordinate to discuss the achievement of the set objectives. Training implications will also be considered at an appraisal interview, both in respect of uplifting poor performance and enhancing satisfactory work. At the meeting comments on overall performance may be made by the reviewer, with an opportunity for the job holder to make his or her comments. This meeting is documented and the form passed to the reviewer's manager for information. The reviewer and the job holder are each provided with a copy.

*2. The rating scheme.* Rating schemes are generally applicable to the manual labour force. A number of performance factors are identified and rated on a sliding scale. Such factors include:

- Quantity of output
- Quality of work
- Knowledge
- Teamwork
- Attendance

The ratings are made on a five-level scale — unsatisfactory, fair, good, very good and exceptional — and these are discussed with the employees. Where any performance factor is considered by management to be unacceptable, the required standards are reiterated by the manager and agreement is reached on the steps required to improve performance. A rating is also made on overall performance, and the employee is given the opportunity to make comments. The review is then documented and signed by the employee, the reviewer and by the reviewer's manager.

Figure 8.2a gives an example of a performance review form. On this form the employee's manager will tick the appropriate box relevant to the employee's performance. The descriptions of the factors can, if necessary, be omitted from the review form with the manager only having the descriptions to provide guidance. The reverse side of the form (Figure 8.2b) is used to note the agreed steps required to

Name:............................................... Position:.................................... Review date:.....................

| Factors | *Quantity*<br>Consider output of satisfactory work during review period | *Quality*<br>Extent to which work meets quality requirements | *Knowledge*<br>Extent to which employee has the knowledge to do the job | *Teamwork*<br>How well the employee works with others | *Attendance*<br>Level of employee absence and punctuality | *Overall*<br>Consider overall performance of employee |
|---|---|---|---|---|---|---|
| *Unsatisfactory*<br>Performance is deficient enough to justify termination unless improved | Output inadequate to retain in job without improvement | Quality too poor to retain in job without improvement | Knowledge inadequate to retain in job without improvement | Uncooperative, improvement essential to retain job | Frequently late and/or absent, improvement required to retain job | Unsatisfactory performance, must improve to retain job |
| *Fair*<br>Below requirements for the job and must improve to be satisfactory | Output below job requirements | Work below standard quality requirements | Lacks required knowledge for job | Works reasonably well but occasionally uncooperative | Absence/lateness levels higher than average | Does not meet requirements of job in all respects, needs improvement |
| *Good*<br>Meets the job requirements. This is the basic acceptable standard of performance | Output satisfies job requirements | Work satisfies quality requirements | Knowledge satisfies ordinary requirements | Cooperative and flexible employee | Attendance and lateness levels acceptable | Meets standard required in all job requirements |
| *Very Good*<br>Beyond the ordinary require-ments for good performance | Output exceeds job requirements | Quality high, work very well done | Very well informed on all phases of work in job | Works well with others | Rarely absent or late | Ahead of standard require-ments in job |
| *Exceptional*<br>Performance is excellent, approaching the best possible for the job | Unusual speed and volume of output | Unusual accuracy, thoroughness and effectiveness | Exceptionally well informed on all phases of work in job | Works extremely well with others, enthusiastic and responsible | Never absent or late | Well ahead of standard requirements in job |

*Figure 8.2a. Performance review – manual employees.*

| |
|---|
| Action required to improve performance: |
| Employee's comments on performance review: |
| Employee's signature:..................................Date:.................. <br> Reviewer's signature:..................................Date:.................. <br> Reviewer's manager's signature ..................................Date:.................. |

*Figure 8.2b. Comments on performance review.*

improve performance, to note any comments made by the employee, and for the signatures of the employee, reviewer and the reviewer's manager.

### *Review of employee potential*

Whilst performance review appraisal is clearly a line management responsibility, the review of employee potential involves other managers in the assessment process. Sometimes line managers are negative in their assessment of employees because having promotable subordinates causes problems of recruitment and training in the event of promotion. But this is not the only pitfall. Keeping good people down also leads to other difficulties: the employees become frustrated and discontented and work suffers. The line manager is not always the best person to evaluate a subordinate's suitability for a different type of job, so other managers or specialized personnel need to be involved.

When looking at good performance, managers need to identify the employee's underlying qualities and skills, taking into account indi-

tudes. They then relate them to future jobs for which the employee might be considered. Assessment opportunities are improved if individuals are exposed to work of a different type from that normally undertaken. Cover for holidays and absence creates such opportunities.

Some contribution to assessment can be gained from self-assessment, and individuals can be invited to assess their own potential. An obvious weakness is that the information will be subjective. In practice self-assessments can be widely different from objective assessment, both in under-estimation of potential as well as in excessive optimism.

In the process of appraising employee potential, care must be taken that the employee's aspirations are not raised unrealistically. The question 'Do you want promotion?' usually brings the response of 'Yes'. It is better for a manager first to discuss with the employee his or her strengths and weaknesses, the type of work that is enjoyed, and relocation, if it is relevant. Ultimately the manager has to make an informed judgement on the employee's suitability for other work.

If it is considered that an employee is not promotable, the person should be told. If the employee has potential, this should be made known, but it has to be made clear at the same time that there is no guarantee of promotion: opportunities may simply not arise or other potential candidates may be preferred.

Documentation of the appraisal interview should incorporate the employee's own views, and the manager's assessments in respect of short-term (12—24 months) potential change of employment, and longer term (3—5 years). The document should also state clearly what actions in respect of training, education and job experience are considered necessary to achieve the potential.

For senior personnel the level of skill necessary to appraise potential is not always readily available in-house, and candidates may be sent to an external assessment centre. Psychometric tests, simulation exercises and interviews are used to obtain the information on which to base an assessment of the employee's potential.

### *Reward review*

There is a third appraisal system called 'reward review' but its application is limited. The reward review is held at a different time from the performance review: the purpose of the review meeting is to link the employee's performance to pay. The individual employee will be aware of his or her performance, and is presumed also to be aware of the company's remuneration policy. It is the manager's responsibility to advise the employee of his or her pay level by reference to the company's reward formulae and levels of payment. The manager must ensure that the employee understands fully the structure of reward payments.

## The Way to Do It

***Question: What are the practical stages to an appraisal interview?***

In the context of day-to-day business the appraisal interview is not constructive. It has to be dealt with to keep the business on the right lines, but for busy managers the appraisal interview is often seen as a necessary but unwanted chore, for which time is reluctantly found. Despite pressures of time, the interview itself must not be treated lightly. Preparation is essential although it need not take a long time.

A helpful checklist of appraisal action is as follows:

- *Invite employee to complete pre-interview form.* Vital information for the appraisal interviewer is the employee's perception of his or her own performance. A useful document is the pre-interview form illustrated in Figure 8.3. The employee should be asked to complete this document and send it to the appraiser seven days before the interview.
- *Read the person's job description.* The purpose is to check whether the job has changed over the review period, or is likely to change in the coming review period.
- *Review available evidence of performance over the review period.* What can be quantified? What are the factors affecting performance that are within the control of the employee? Are there other factors that are beyond the employee's control?
- *Arrange the date, time and place of the interview.* Ensure that the room is free of interruptions.
- *Prepare the appraisal interview plan.*
- *Explain the purpose of the interview.* Employees are likely to be apprehensive and feel threatened. A few 'neutral' words are relaxing and reassuring.
- *Select an item of behaviour for praise.* It is not essential that the activity singled out is for outstanding and exceptional performance. This may not exist. Recognition of even an everyday act performed diligently is motivating.
- *Invite self-assessment from the employee.* Careful prompting with open and leading questions secures the employee's perception of general performance, progress and perceived barriers to successful

Complete this form and the evaluation of performance on the Performance Review Objective Form. Send both forms to your appraiser at least seven days before the interview.

---

*Performance*

1. In relation to your job description, key objectives and evaluation of performance, make comments on your general performance over the review period:

..........................................................................................

..........................................................................................

..........................................................................................

..........................................................................................

..........................................................................................

2. What suggestions do you have for improving your own performance?

..........................................................................................

..........................................................................................

..........................................................................................

..........................................................................................

..........................................................................................

3. Are there any changes you can suggest to your present job to provide greater job satisfaction?

..........................................................................................

..........................................................................................

..........................................................................................

..........................................................................................

..........................................................................................

4. If you are interested in your career development do you have any suggestions as to how your career might develop?

..........................................................................................

..........................................................................................

..........................................................................................

..........................................................................................

..........................................................................................

5. Arising from questions 2, 3 and 4, do you recognize any education training or experience needs?

..........................................................................................

..........................................................................................

..........................................................................................

..........................................................................................

..........................................................................................

| |
|---|
| Employee's name ........................... Position ........................... |
| *Manager's comments prior to interview* (Copies of this form and the Performance Review Objectives form to be available at interview as basis for discussion) |
| ......................................................................................... |
| ......................................................................................... |
| ......................................................................................... |
| ......................................................................................... |
| ......................................................................................... |
| ......................................................................................... |
| ......................................................................................... |
| ......................................................................................... |
| ......................................................................................... |
| Manager's signature ........................... Date ........................... |

*Figure 8.3. Pre-interview form: performance appraisal.*

general performance, progress and perceived barriers to successful development. A useful document used with manual employees is the performance review illustrated in Figure 8.2a. The employee should be asked in discussion with the interviewer to agree where he or she falls within the matrix. One tick is placed in each of the vertical columns reflecting the level of performance from unsatisfactory to exceptional.

- *Agree achievements.*
- *Agree deficiencies.* Discuss in detail where the employee has not met the set targets.
- *Proclaim and confirm company and departmental objectives.*
- *Agree fresh individual targets for the new review period.*
- *Reconcile any divergence of interests.* The manager must be sure to identify areas of stress arising within the work environment or from the employee's personal life that can be a source of conflict. It is important, too, that part-time interests that might intrude are known.
- *Note any training required.*
- *Review the main points.*
- *Allow the interviewee to summarize.*
- *End on a note of confidence.*

A good example comes from RHM Plc. It acquired a company which previously had not used a performance appraisal system. In introducing the system there was initial management resistance. Apprehension particularly arose in the areas of key objectives and the standards of performance required. Managers who in the past had little or no exposure to a job description were now having to come to terms with clear job descriptions, specific accountability and set standards of performance.

The process was painful and some managers left the organization, unable to accept the new disciplines. At the end of the first year management performance was reviewed, and new objectives set. The response of management was positive. One manager commented: 'In ten years working in the company only in the last year have I known what was expected of me. I now know how the company rates my performance. I have agreed my training needs and I am determined to improve my individual performance.' The year-on-year performance of the company under the RHM umbrella improved significantly.

## Influences

### *Question: What are the contributory factors to poor performance?*

In simple terms poor performance means that performance levels are not up to the set standards. But the contributory reasons are not necessarily simple and straightforward; nor is poor performance always easily detected.

On the shop floor, with employees working under constant supervision, poor performance is easily seen when the product quality drops or output falls. With salesmen in the field the situation is very different: sales can be lost due to poor presentational skills, through inadequate communication, or for a variety of other reasons. Poor sales performance is not always immediately perceived.

To manage poor performers initial action is necessary to identify the contributory factors, distinguishing between symptom and cause. Factors that are measurable include:

### *Absenteeism and lateness*

Are certain employees habitually absent or late? Are there patterns to the absence or lateness for particular days of the week or particular weeks of the year? Is the absence of short duration, covered by self-certification, or is the absence for a term longer than a week and covered by a doctor's certificate?

Carefully documented records are essential.

### *Quality of work*

If the employee is not producing work to the appropriate standard, there may be a pattern to the lack of quality. Are there particular areas of work that are unsatisfactory, whilst other areas are fine? It is necessary to ascertain whether poor quality occurs on certain days and not on others.

### *Quantity of work*

If the employee is doing less work than is required one reason may be lack of training. Another reason could be that the employee is unfit. It is necessary to establish whether the workers have control over the amount of work to be done.

### *Behaviour*

Employees may exhibit unacceptable behaviour. Perhaps an employee has problems with other workers and they are reluctant to work with him or her. Do members of the public complain about employee attitudes? From time to time certain employees can be a problem to management or are known to stir up trouble.

### *General appearance*

It is important that all staff in contact with customers and members of the public create a good image. Within the parameters of their particular work they must be neat and tidy. Dirt and indifference to appearance undoubtedly reflect attitudes that signal poor commitment to work standards.

Isolated cases of poor performance do not necessarily give cause for concern. Employees in the category of poor performers are those whose performance over a reasonable period of time is consistently below standard, so it is essential that managers constantly assess performance. Systems to measure absence, lateness, customer complaints, returned goods, scrap rates, etc., over say twelve-monthly periods must be established.

There are a number of causes of poor performance outlined below.

### *Lack of ability or lack of knowledge*

Performance suffers when employees lack ability or knowledge. With new employees it is expected that performance may be below normal standards. However, if after training and a reasonable period at work their performance is still poor, ability and knowledge must be investigated. Particular care should be taken to identify whether poor performance might be due to an ability or knowledge exceeding that required for the job.

### *Stress*

All employees at some time experience stress. In one aspect it is beneficial in increasing motivation, but when the level of stress increases people feel threatened. There may be physiological changes, ranging from headaches through to more serious physical disorders. As a result of stress people react in a manner different from their normal behaviour pattern. Some panic, and cease to think rationally; others become defensive or aggressive.

Stress in the workplace is caused by a number of factors:

- Boredom.
- No feedback given to employees as to how they are performing.
- Poor workplace layout, so that staff cannot find needed tools and materials.
- Poorly controlled environment with inadequate or excessive ventilation or lighting.
- Inadequate job instruction.
- Insecurity arising from uncertainty and threat of redundancy.

Individuals are affected in different ways by different stress factors, but the outcome is behaviour change. Any such change is a signal to the manager that performance is at risk.

### *Alcoholism and drug abuse*

Employees who are heavy drinkers or drug users are often poor performers, with poor performance records. Drug-taking is on the increase but alcoholism is still the biggest problem. It occurs at all levels within the organization, and there are easily recognizable signals by which the heavy drinker can be recognized:

- Smell of drink on breath or attempts to disguise the smell.
- The need to have a drink before any important event.
- Drinking alone often in places not normally visited by work colleagues.
- Drinking faster than work colleagues.
- Drinking larger measures.

For the drug users there are recognizable symptoms too:

- Sudden changes in behaviour.
- The person increasingly becomes confused and irritable.
- Fluctuations in the employee's energy levels.
- Deterioration in relationships with other employees.

### *Medical problems*

Employee performance can be affected by medical problems that may or may not be known to the employer. Where known, management has to be aware of how these problems can affect performance. Whenever possible employees should be transferred to other work from which there is minimal loss of performance, or no loss at all.

Initially, with a deterioration in performance by individual employees, a manager can only surmise that the cause may be due to ill health. In such cases the employee should be asked to see his or her own doctor or to visit the company nurse or doctor. Company medical personnel are well placed to advise management in effective utilization of employees suffering from medical problems. In their absence companies have to rely on the advice of the employee's doctor.

### *Other employees*

For most employees starting work or a new job there is the immediate problem of joining a group of strangers. Getting on with this group is essential to good performance. The employee needs to be accepted by the group, and without that acceptance performance is very likely to suffer.

The most common reason for rejection within the group is that the employee sees himself or herself as different from the others. This takes a number of forms:

- The employee is either better or less well educated than the rest of the work group.
- The employee's accent is different from the group. This is particularly significant where the accent implies higher social standing.
- Employees are of different race, nationality, colour or religion.
- The age of the employee differs greatly from the ages of other group members.
- The supervisor is a person who was recently promoted from a group that he or she is now supervising.

### *Family and domestic problems*

All employees at some time experience family and domestic problems that affect their performance. The most common problems here are death, divorce, separation, difficulties with children, moving house and debt.

## Providing Help

### *Question: How does the counselling interview help to resolve the problems of poor performance?*

Unless an interview is specifically requested by an employee, the need for counselling is usually indicated by a fall-off in performance. The purpose of counselling is to establish the reason for poor performance. It is a behavioural problem — only after the true reasons are established can successful future action be determined.

Generally there are two reasons for poor performance:

- Interpersonal problems, which may arise within the workplace or outside.
- Work-related problems. There can be a variety of causes: the problems may be due to lack of training, absence of clear objectives, ill-defined performance levels, poor environmental conditions or lack of motivation.

Uncovering the underlying causes of poor performance in the counselling interview is not always easy, particularly when the reasons are personal. Employees are usually reluctant to divulge information about adverse personal circumstances, but it is essential that the information is obtained: without it further action cannot logically be planned.

The counselling interview differs dramatically from the employment selection interview. The difference lies in the approach that has to be adopted.

### *Steps of the counselling interview*

*Step 1.* Check to see whether any standards have been set for the job. They are either incorporated in the job description or specifically set for the performance appraisal.

*Step 2.* Agree standards with the employee. If there are no formal objectives the employee should be asked what he or she understands the standards to be for an average employee. The manager then gives his/her perception of such standards, and makes sure that agreement is reached on the appropriate standards.

*Step 3.* Identify by discussion the difference between the agreed standards and the employee's own performance levels. At this stage the reasons for the difference are not probed: this is done at the next stage. Step 3 aims to identify the number of factors on which the employee fails to meet the standards and the extent of that failure.

Discussion on individual factors at this stage may result in the employee taking a defensive stance.

*Step 4.* Discuss and agree the implication of poor performance for the employee, his or her colleagues and for the company. As an example, if the employee is absent frequently, what are the repercussions? The employee may suffer loss of pay; work colleagues have a requirement to undertake extra work; the organization defaults on its level of customer service. The reasons are probed. The manager needs to be supportive, particularly if it becomes clear that adverse domestic or personal circumstances are contributory factors.

*Step 5.* Agree with the employee the responsibility for improving performance. It is important to get the employee to accept total or partial responsibility for improvement. The counselling manager should be prepared to help but any action has to follow on from the employee's commitment.

*Step 6.* Summarize the actions to be taken by the employee and the actions the manager has agreed to undertake. The timescale is defined, and the commitment agreed for immediate implementation of the change.

Good managers with good interviewing skills should be able to carry out counselling in relation to work-related problems. Good managers also recognize that in certain circumstances the help they can offer is limited, and professional counselling help may be advisable from a doctor, psychologist or other specialist. It may be appropriate to suggest that the employee contacts one of the organizations specializing in particular problems. The following can help:

Relate — National Marriage Guidance
Herbert Gray College
Little Church Street
Rugby CV21 3AP
Tel. 0788-573241

Alcoholics Anonymous
P.O. Box 1
Stonebow House
Stonebow
York YO1 2NJ
Tel. 0904-644026 and 071-352 3001

Cruse — Bereavement Care
126 Sheen Road
Richmond
Surrey TW9 1UR
Tel. 081-940 4818

Carers National Association
29 Chilworth Mews
London W2 3RG
Tel. 071-724 7776

Samaritans
46 Marshall Street
London W1V 1LR
Tel. (Help line) 071-734 2800

Wash — Women Against Sexual Harassment
242 Pentonville Road
London N1 9UN
Tel. 071-833 0222

## All That Can Be Done

***Question: What are the parameters of disciplinary procedure?***

For some employees disciplinary action is necessary before an improvement in work performance occurs. Following such disciplinary action, failure to improve inevitably leads to dismissal. Infrequently, an action of the employee construed as gross misconduct, such as major theft or fraud, results in instant dismissal.

Disciplinary rules and procedures are necessary to promoting fairness and order in the treatment of employees. The positive aspect of discipline is improvement in performance.

In any organization there are company rules — formal and informal, written and unwritten. It is not reasonable to assume that all employees are aware of those company rules that apply to them. The rules should be in writing and a copy given to each employee. All new employees should receive their copy as part of the induction process.

It is recommended that companies without written rules should take action to produce them. It is suggested too that for companies whose written rules have been in existence for some time, such rules are reviewed. All managers should be involved in the preparation of company rules to reach agreement on the level of discipline to be applied — i.e. from minor misconduct through more serious misconduct to gross misconduct resulting in dismissal.

The rules inevitably vary from company to company. A golden rule is that they be written in a positive manner, i.e. 'You will...' rather than 'You will not...' An example of common company rules is illustrated below.

It is a requirement of the Employment Protection (Consolidation) Act 1978 that all employees must be notified of any disciplinary rules that apply to them. This is to be enacted by giving the employees copies, or advising where the rules can be seen. Employees have the right to appeal against a disciplinary decision, and it is necessary that the employees know of the appeal procedure. An example of Company Rules and Disciplinary Procedure Notice is given below.

---

**Company Rules**

1. You are required to report and be available for work at the time stated in your terms and conditions of employment.

2. You must observe the stated lunch break.

3. It is a requirement that you have the approval of your manager before leaving your workplace during your contracted working hours.

4. You are required to respect both the Company and other employees' property by:

   (a) not abusing or wilfully damaging Company or employees' property.
   (b) using Company property only for Company business.
   (c) using work time only for Company work.

5. You are required to respect fellow employees by:

   (a) not intimidating or threatening other employees either by physical violence, bad language, or disorderly conduct.
   (b) following all reasonable instructions given by your manager.
   (c) not bringing alcohol onto premises for consumption or being under the influence of alcohol or drugs.

6. You are required to protect Company and employee facilities by:

(a) smoking only in designated smoking areas.
(b) following safe working procedures and only using authorized equipment.
(c) in the event of fire following the fire alarm procedures.

7. You are required to be truthful and accurate when completing self-certification forms, holiday requests and other Company forms.

8. You are required to treat information acquired during the course of your job as confidential.

---

## Notice of Disciplinary Procedure

### Aim

To ensure that the treatment of employees by the Company is conducted in a fair and well ordered manner.

### Objectives

The procedure is designed to help and encourage all employees to maintain set standards of conduct, attendance and job performance. Disciplinary procedure is to be read in conjunction with the Company Rules.

### Principles

1. No disciplinary action is to be taken against an employee until the case has been fully investigated.
2. An employee subject to a disciplinary hearing will be advised of the nature of the complaint. He or she is then given the opportunity to state his or her case before any decision is made.
3. At any stage in the procedure the employee has the right to be accompanied by a trade union representative, employee representative or work colleague.
4. An employee has the right to appeal against any disciplinary penalty imposed.

### Procedure

Minor offences are to be dealt with informally. Where the matter is more serious the following procedures are used:

*Stage 1 — Oral warning*
If conduct or performance does not meet acceptable standards the employee will be given a formal oral warning. This warning will give the reason for the warning, the improvement required and the right to appeal. A note of the warning is kept for a period of three months and then discarded, subject to satisfactory conduct and performance.

*Stage 2 — First written warning*
If the offence is deemed more serious than that generating an oral warning, or a further misconduct occurs, a first written warning is given to the employee by the manager. This document gives details of the complaint, the improvement required, the timescale, and the employee's right to appeal.

The written warning remains in force for a period of six months. After that period, subject to satisfactory conduct and performance, the warning is spent.

*Stage 3 — Final written warning or suspension*
If conduct or performance is still unsatisfactory or if the misconduct is sufficiently serious, a final written warning will be given to the employee by his or her manager. This document gives details of the complaint, the improvement required, the timescale, and the employee's right to appeal. This warning remains in force for a period of 12 months. After that period, subject to satisfactory conduct and performance, it is discarded. In certain circumstances, consideration will be given to imposing a penalty of suspension without pay, up to a maximum of five working days.

*Stage 4 — Dismissal*
If conduct or performance is still unsatisfactory, or the conduct is classified as gross misconduct, then dismissal will result. The employee's manager, after seeking approval from senior management, will implement the dismissal by providing the employee with written reasons for dismissal, the date of termination, and stating the employee's right to appeal.

## Gross misconduct

The following offences are given as examples of gross misconduct:

- Fighting or assaulting another employee.
- Theft, fraud, dishonesty.

- Deliberate damage to the property of the company or other employees.
- Incapability through alcohol or illegal drugs.
- Serious act of negligence.
- Serious breach of confidentiality.
- Serious breach of health and safety regulations.
- Unauthorized entry to computer records.

Employees accused of gross misconduct are immediately suspended from work on full pay up to a maximum of five working days whilst the company investigates the offence. If the company is satisfied that gross misconduct has occurred the result is summary dismissal without notice or payment in lieu of notice.

### Appeal procedure

An employee wishing to appeal against a disciplinary decision must inform the Personnel Manager within three working days. A senior manager will hear all appeals and his or her decision will be final.

## Practical Steps

***Question: What are the stages of disciplinary action?***

The diagram below shows the stages involved in taking disciplinary action:

| | | |
|---|---|---|
| Minor misconduct | —— *Stage 1* —— | First oral warning |
| More serious misconduct or further minor misconduct | —— *Stage 2* —— | First written warning |
| More serious misconduct or further serious misconduct | —— *Stage 3* —— | Final written warning or suspension |
| Gross misconduct or continuing further offences | —— *Stage 4* —— | Dismissal |

Each stage can exert significant influence on employee performance.

### *Informal warnings*

An informal warning is often the best way to achieve improvement in employee performance where offences of minor misconduct occur. This on-the-job reprimand indicates unequivocally that the conduct or performance is unacceptable. The warning should be given by the employee's immediate superior, and there is a structure to the warning irrespective of the industry or to the manager's experience. The informal warning should:

- Be in private.
- Be out of view and earshot of other employees.
- Be brief.
- Invite the employee's explanation.
- Explain concisely what the employee has done that is unacceptable.
- Formally advise the employee that the conversation is to be treated as an informal verbal warning.

### *Formal disciplinary action*

Before the decision is made to take formal disciplinary action it is essential that all the circumstances are carefully assessed. It is particularly important that the standards expected be compared with employee performance. Certain questions should be asked:

- Is the employee aware that his or her behaviour is unacceptable?
- Are there relevant rules, written or unwritten?
- If such rules exist, are they enforced regularly?
- Was the employee aware of such rules before the unacceptable performance or behaviour took place?

When, after consideration of the evidence, it is decided that disciplinary action is necessary, the following four steps should be followed:

*Step 1.* Advise the employee in advance of the allegations. Inform the employee of his or her right to be accompanied at the interview.

*Step 2.* Conduct the disciplinary interview giving the employee opportunity to state his or her case.

*Step 3.* Adjourn the interview to consider the facts. If disciplinary action is to be taken, decide at what level it is to be — oral, first written, final written, suspension or dismissal.

*Step 4.* Take the appropriate disciplinary action. Inform the employee of the appeals procedure.

## Practical Steps

### *Question: What are the ingredients of good discipline management?*

For many disciplinary interviews that do not demand immediate action, management can select a time that is convenient to the manager. For employees certain problems relating to time-keeping, poor performance or attitude develop over a period of time. By arranging a discipline interview at a time to suit the manager, there is an opportunity for the manager to investigate the circumstances and gather appropriate evidence in preparation for the interview.

The timing of an interview is often important, particularly if the manager anticipates problems or emotional scenes. It may be expedient to arrange the interview at the end of the employee's working day, so that there is a 'cooling-off' period before the employee has to return to work. Friday is a particularly effective day, allowing the weekend for the employee to reflect on the implications of the disciplinary interview.

As with the informal interview, there is a structure to be followed:

- When documentation is used as evidence, it must be available at the interview. When the issue is complex, the employee should be provided with the documentary evidence prior to the disciplinary interview.
- Any witnesses to be called must be advised in advance and attendance confirmed.
- Previous disciplinary action or actions should be recited at the interview.
- An explanation for failure to improve or for the reoccurrence of misconduct is requested from the employee.
- It should be established whether there are personal or mitigating circumstances.
- After all the evidence has been presented and the defence of the employee heard, the meeting should be adjourned for decision-making.
- When the meeting is reconvened the employee is advised of the decision.
- The appeals procedure should be explained to the employee if he or she is dissatisfied with the decision.

- A letter must be sent to the employee confirming the substance of the disciplinary interview decision.

### *Documentation*

To ensure fairness and consistency, all formal disciplinary action must be documented. This necessity is illustrated by cases of dismissal of employees who then appeal against dismissal to an industrial tribunal. The documentation will be invaluable as support for the company's argument of fair dismissal.

In the circumstances of an informal warning or on-the-job reprimand, all that is necessary is for the line manager to place on file a note containing the date, name of employee and the nature of the reprimand.

With a formal verbal warning a letter confirming details of the warning should be placed in the employee's personnel file. The details must include:

- The date of the warning.
- The reason for the warning.
- The improvement required.
- The period for which the warning is to remain in force.
- Confirmation that the employee was advised of the right to appeal.

For first and final written warnings the documented warning is given to the employee and a copy is given to his or her representative. A further copy is retained in the employee's personnel file. The warning letters confirm that a disciplinary interview was held and gives details of the outcome. The letters advise the employee of:

- The nature of the unsatisfactory conduct or performance.
- The improvement in performance or conduct that is required, and the timescale.
- The consequences if improvement is not forthcoming.
- The period during which the warning remains effective.
- Details the action necessary if the employee wishes to appeal.

Where the employee is dismissed, following a disciplinary interview, the letter confirming the dismissal should state:

- Reference to any relevant previous warnings.
- The reason for the dismissal.
- The date of the dismissal.

- Whether payment is to be made in lieu of notice, the period of the notice and the amount of monies to be paid.
- In the case of dismissal for gross misconduct the employee is advised that no notice or pay in lieu of notice is given.
- Details of the action necessary in the event of the employee wishing to appeal.

Copies of the letter should be given to the employee and the employee's representative, and a copy retained in his or her personnel file.

## Summary

*Question:* What are the major systems of appraisal used to monitor employee performance?

*Answer:* There are two major systems of appraisal: the performance review and the review of employee potential. In addition there is a reward review but this has a less frequent application.

*Question:* What are the practical stages of an appraisal interview?

*Answer:* The first appraisal stage lies in preparation for the interview. Administrative details of time, place and venue are completed; documentation is read. An interview plan is prepared as a control document. The interview proceeds from an explanation of the interview purpose, through employee self-assessment, to agreement on performance levels, agreement on positive future action and the setting and agreement of future objectives to be met.

*Question:* What are the contributory factors to poor performance?

*Answer:* Poor performance is expressed through absenteeism and lateness, unacceptable quality, or quantity of work, improper behaviour and sloppy appearance. The major causes of poor performance are lack of ability or lack of knowledge, stress, alcoholism and drug abuse, medical problems, dissonance with other employees, and family or domestic problems.

*Question:* How does the counselling interview help to resolve the problems of poor performance?

*Answer:* The purpose of counselling is to establish the reason for poor performance and help to resolve the problems. The problems may be interpersonal or work-related.

The counselling interview is structured to identify and agree acceptable performance standards; to identify the difference between actual and desired performance; the action from both sides necessary to achieve change; and to secure commitment from the employee.

*Question:* What are the parameters of disciplinary procedure?

*Answer:* Disciplinary action comprises the steps to be taken to ensure that performance and procedure within an organization conform to the standards laid down within the company rules.

*Question:* What are the stages of disciplinary action?

*Answer:* There are four stages of disciplinary action: (1) first oral warning; (2) first written warning; (3) final written warning; and (4) dismissal.

*Question:* What are the ingredients of good discipline management?

*Answer:* A well-prepared interview plays an important role in discipline management. Interview timing is planned to fit within a management schedule, and when appropriate to allow the employee a 'cooling-off' period before his or her return to work. Another important ingredient is sound documentation recording step by step the sequence of events and actions taken.

# 9

# WANTING TO WORK TO THE LIMIT

Before reading this chapter please answer the following questions. The material is worked through in the text. Questions and answers are given together at the end of the chapter in the form of a summary.

## Questions

- What management homework precedes effective motivation?
- How effective are suggestion schemes?
- What suggestion scheme format creates the best opportunities for savings and improvement?
- What are the motivational aspects of teamwork?
- What role does team briefing play in teamwork?
- How do leadership skills influence motivation?
- How is the impact of 'downsizing' softened?
- When mass redundancy is a reality, how is the change best managed?

## Preparation

### *Question: What management homework precedes effective motivation?*

A well-motivated workforce has commitment. Employees manifest their commitment by:

- Working to meet the organization's goals.
- Exerting effort beyond that specified in the job contract.
- Wanting to remain in the employment of the organization.
- Taking pride in group achievement.

Application of the management activities set out in the previous chapters assists employees in wanting to work. There are other activities too, discussed below, that can play a significant role in gaining employee commitment.

But the starting point to motivation that really gets results is finding out what employees think. Carry out an attitude survey! This should be done on a regular basis, preferably with no longer than two years between surveys. Many large companies — IBM is one known to the authors — carry out regular attitude surveys. They allow management to assess and understand the level of employee morale, to identify the nature of satisfaction, and to identify trends in perception. The survey provides a basis for discussion at all levels within the company, and allows management to take appropriate action whenever necessary.

One of the important findings of the attitude survey lies in giving management an understanding of employee priorities. An example is in relation to company benefits. One company in the North of England spent a considerable amount of money on resurfacing the company car park and painting lines to demarcate private car spaces. The attitude survey revealed that although employees welcomed the improvement in car parking facilities, they would have preferred an improvement of the catering facilities. Such action would have cost the company less money.

Another benefit of an attitude survey, an important benefit, is that it increases the involvement of the employees. The simple process of asking employees for their views invariably raises morale.

In large companies, attitude surveys are usually carried out by the personnel function. Where there is no in-house expertise the work can be done by commercial consultants.

In either case the organization should form a project team to oversee the survey. Although it is more cost-effective to conduct surveys in-house, the organization may lack experience in survey techniques and employees may doubt the anonymity of the survey questionnaire if analysed internally. Consultants have an advantage in the ability to compare results (anonymously) with other client surveys to highlight results that differ significantly.

It has been found that the best results, in terms of percentage response rate, are obtained if all employees are invited to participate. Where sheer numbers prevent this, it is recommended that many more participants are used than the minimum number statistically acceptable as a sample.

Attitude surveys are invariably questionnaire-based. They ask questions on every aspect for which the company seeks information. The most common are employee attitudes towards:

- Customers.
- Potential customers.
- The company's distribution channels.
- Management style.
- Management values.
- The employees themselves.
- Terms and conditions of work.
- Promotion opportunities.
- Working environment.
- Social environment.
- Perks.
- Company performance.
- Company image.

To ensure acceptability of the questionnaire to both company and employees, a pilot study should be undertaken. The respondents' reaction to the draft questionnaire is a useful pointer to inadvertent gaps or to weighted questions. It is usually found that respondents enjoy completing a 'good' questionnaire.

The time allowed to complete a questionnaire is also important. In practical terms the design should require a time of 30—60 minutes, with between 100 and 250 questions to be answered. It is important that questions should be answered quickly to reflect the 'gut reaction' of respondents.

The most successful rating scale ranges from 'Strongly Agree' to 'Strongly Disagree'. The scale should have an even number of boxes to avoid respondents automatically choosing the middle one. It is useful for spaces to be left so that respondents can write comments of their own.

Once survey questionnaires are issued the time allowed for completion must be a careful balance between too much — with the danger of being overlooked — and too little — leading to a poor response rate. One to two weeks is a reasonable period.

For survey answers to have any value they must represent the true feelings of employees — not views that the employees think management wants to hear. For this reason all responses should be anonymous. When groups are identified there should be a minimum of six persons to prevent the identification of individual respondents. Extensive advance publicity for any survey is essential in preparing respondents for the forthcoming event with clear explanations of what is about to take place.

Completion of the survey administration is not the end of the exercise. Much value derives from the discussions that follow when the results of the survey are communicated by management to the workforce, in a series of meetings. Surveys will give clear indications of issues causing concern. Generally, employees will seek to know what action the company proposes to take as a result of the views expressed. A prompt response is advisable to maintain and build on the goodwill created during the survey.

## Trying Hard
### *Question: How effective are suggestion schemes?*

Suggestion schemes invite ideas from employees. If the ideas result in cost savings or improve safety, the employee should be financially rewarded. There are other benefits to organizations, such as:

- A reward offered to employees for good suggestions motivates many employees to search for improvements.
- A company-wide suggestion scheme enables employees to bypass their managers if it is considered that a suggestion is unlikely to be favourably received by a particular manager.
- Employees who are creative and lateral thinkers come to the attention of management.
- A poor response to a suggestions scheme may give an indication of poor morale or of other problems requiring attention.
- Successful schemes invariably encourage a climate of positive change within the organization.

Tom Peters, the American management writer, lecturing in London, said that in his country it was fashionable to give great publicity hype to the most successful employee suggestions. Ideas saving thousands of dollars are loved by everyone: everyone benefits. But, he argued, of monumental importance are the many small implemented decisions of a work team, to move, say, a filing cabinet six inches that has been standing in the way for ten years. Such suggestions are the cement of teamwork, and the foundations of growth and progress.

In 1987 a survey by the United Kingdom Association of Suggestions Schemes (UKASS) found that average savings were £265,000 a year. Four organizations saved more than £1m each in that year. The average participation rate was five suggestions per 100 employees: the average adoption rate was 22 per cent of the suggestions received.

## A Winning Formula

### *Question: What suggestion scheme format creates the best opportunities for savings and improvement?*

Schemes should be such that all employees are eligible to participate, provided that the idea put forward does not fall within the employee's own area of responsibility. The test is to ask two questions:

- Could the change be made on the employee's own responsibility?
- Will the employee be open to criticism by management for not having made the change?

If the answer is 'No' in each case, the suggestion should be eligible. Suggestion schemes can also be extended to include company suppliers. For example, Rover Cars have a special scheme for some of their suppliers with a Metro car being offered each year for the best suggestion.

At the introduction of a suggestion scheme a Suggestion Scheme Committee should be set up, comprising not more than six members with diverse experience. Where trade unions are recognized it is usual to have a trade union representative on the committee. In practice, the company designs the suggestion form. Suggestions are submitted to the scheme secretary who indicates how long the assessment will take. Before consideration of the suggestion by the committee, the suggester's name should be replaced by a number to ensure that evaluation is anonymous.

Suggestions committees can make three types of awards:

- Interest awards for ideas that will not be implemented. These are

ideas that have some intrinsic merit and reflect meritorious effort on the part of the employee.
- Valued awards for suggestions leading to quantifiable savings. Such awards are usually a straight percentage of the savings.
- Special awards for ideas related to safety or the environment, where savings are not easily quantified.

It is for organizations to determine their own reward structure. A recent survey showed a wide range of awards. Companies must also take heed of Inland Revenue rules in respect of the tax treatment of suggestion awards. Awards are tax-free provided that:

- There is a formally constituted scheme open to all employees on equal terms.
- Suggestions are outside the scope of the employee's normal duties.
- Rewards, other than interest awards, are only made following a decision to implement the suggestion.
- The award does not exceed 50 per cent of the first year's financial benefit or 10 per cent of the financial benefits over a five-year period, subject to a maximum of £5,000.
- An interest award should be no more than £25.
- Where a suggestion is put forward by a group the award is divided between them on a reasonable basis.

To be successful suggestion schemes must be well publicized. Companies should use all the communication channels available. The best publicity is to publicize awards but, as with the football pools, suggesters' names should be publicized only with the agreement of the person concerned.

## Added Value

***Question: What are the motivational aspects of teamwork?***

Many companies now follow the Japanese practice in the adoption of the teamwork concept. The philosophy behind teamwork is that all employees work together as a team towards a common goal. The benefits of teamworking are:

- *Flexibility.* Employees within the team are trained to be competent in several if not all of the tasks constituting their area of responsibility. This enables team members to move from job to job as required to maximize efficiency and productivity. When individual team members are absent, disruption to work is minimized by members providing cover.

- *Work quality.* Quality improvement is achieved within the team, as members work together in a process to pass on good products or services to the next team in the operation. It is a self-motivating system. Because there is 'ownership' of the process and recognition that the next team as an internal customer will accept only top quality work, the accepted aims of quality improvement and quality control are implemented. In some companies the responsibility for quality is formally taken away from the quality control department and given to the team.
- *Empowerment.* Within teams members are responsible for organizing and structuring their own work. This often results in a reorganization of the management structure with a layer of management removed.

  Hardy Spicer Ltd, a division of GKN, changed their production to teamworking from a traditional hierarchical organizational structure. The company reorganized into five distinct operations each run as a semi-autonomous business. The level of the works manager was abolished. Five factory managers were created in place of production managers: deputy factory managers were introduced for each shift to ensure continuity of control. Within each shift the teams are headed by a team leader.

  Companies invariably find that in giving employees greater freedom to organize their own work, those employees show more initiative in resolving problems and in generating quality and production improvements.
- *Composition and size of teams.* The size of teams can vary but for good teamwork they should have between eight and 12 members. The composition will vary from company to company depending on the team's tasks. An important element is the balance of skills. Companies must aim to secure a mix of personal characteristics, practical skills and knowledge. A team with too many strong characters leads to personality clashes. The team should also contain all the skills required to meet its tasks, with back-up skills to meet bottlenecks in production and to cover for absences. Wherever possible the team leader should be competent in performing all the team's tasks.
- *Job satisfaction.* Job rotation within teams should be encouraged to improve job satisfaction and reinforce the competence of each member in performing every task. The extent of job rotation will depend on the degree of cross-skilling or multi-skilling in the team, and the requirement to balance flexibility with efficiency.

Job rotation at the expense of productivity is counterproductive. It is up to team leaders to decide how often jobs are to be rotated.

- *Training.* The requirement to provide training when introducing teamworking must not be overlooked. Teamleaders in particular need extensive training if they are to perform well. Kodak, for example, has a structured training course certified by the National Examination Board of Supervisory Management, involving seven weeks' training over a 21-week period.

## Getting It Right

***Question: What role does team briefing play in teamwork?***

Team briefing is an important aspect of the communication flow within an organization. It is a regular means of keeping employees informed about what is happening in the company. Through the briefings communication flows downwards from top management to the shop floor. At each level there are opportunities for team members to ask questions. There are many benefits from team briefings:

- The manager's position as leader is reinforced. In earlier times, the shop steward was seen as the leader because he or she was communicating the findings of union meetings. Line managers often heard about events in the company for the first time from the shop steward. The introduction of team briefings brought about a change, and the role of leader moved to line management.
- The commitment of employees is increased. The knowledge of targets, how the team/department is doing, how the organization as a whole is performing, gives the workforce a direction. In one team, for example, absenteeism was always a problem. Although employees were counselled individually, the level of absenteeism did not improve. At a team briefing the departmental rate of absenteeism was compared and discussed against the lower general level of absenteeism in the company. Following this meeting the departmental absenteeism rate reduced significantly.
- Team briefings help the company to implement change. Advising the workforce why something needs to be done, how, and when, helps to gain commitment. The employees may not agree with the policy but are more disposed to agree with the proposals if they understand the underlying reason. An example from the paper board industry illustrates this. The company required workers to move into a three-shift system for a three-month period to meet a production order. Management explained that the cost of weekend

working would involve the company in a substantial loss on the order. Turning down the order would antagonize a valued customer at a time when the business climate was difficult and uncertain. When management explained the full circumstances the employees accepted three-shift working.

- Team briefing balances against the grapevine. All organizations have a grapevine that passes instant information, accurate and inaccurate. Established regular briefings can counteract rumour and speculation.

  In one engineering company the workforce stopped work during one day, on hearing of major redundancies through the grapevine. Management called a meeting with the workforce — a practice to which they were not accustomed — to explain that there was no truth in the rumour. The workforce asked for the involvement of their full-time trade union official. Only when he dismissed the threat of redundancies did the employees return to work, some four hours after laying down their tools.
- Enhanced levels of communication are achieved by regular opportunities for employees to ask questions, following team briefings. In one organization employees were briefed on a visit of the chairman, whose schedule included a tour of that division of the company. Several employees asked for a description of the chairman, and a photograph with a brief note on his career was displayed on the company noticeboards. As the chairman had started his career as a craftsman and worked his way up the management ladder, the employees without exception displayed their respect for him. Without this specific knowledge he would have been just another VIP on a factory tour.

In addition to having team briefings on a regular basis, i.e. daily, weekly or monthly, it is useful to choose the same day and time. Everyone then knows that their team briefing is on, say, the last Friday in the month at the start of the working day. Briefings normally should last no more than 30 minutes. If there is a need to communicate especial news, an ad hoc meeting can be called.

The content of a team briefing can be structured on the 'Four Ps' principle:

Progress
Policy
People, and
Points for action.

The essence of team briefing is the core brief, which originates at senior management level and is issued in the form of a document to all briefers. The core brief will account for about 30 per cent of the meeting. Other matters are provided by the team briefer using the principle of the Four Ps to identify matters of relevant interest.

Questions that cannot be answered by the manager conducting a briefing should not be ducked or invented answers supplied. Correct information should be promised and then supplied at the next briefing session. All questions should be recorded, and analysis by management will identify the range and depth of employee concerns.

In some organizations trade unions may object to any communication relating to the terms and conditions of employment, arguing that this is their prerogative.

As with all systems, it is desirable to monitor the effectiveness of team briefing. There are a number of options:

- Higher management might occasionally sit in on the briefing sessions to check that information is passed on accurately and the meetings are conducted efficiently.
- A team briefing coordinator can be appointed to monitor consistency and to collect and analyse all feedback forms.
- Managers may seek feedback on system effectiveness by talking to employees individually or in groups.

## Positive Input

***Question: How do leadership skills influence motivation?***

Motivation is not a specific action: it is the result of specific actions. Most competent acts of leadership contribute to a motivated workforce — a workforce in which every employee strives to work to the limits of his or her capability. There is a structure to the leadership of a well-motivated team, made up of four discrete steps (See Figure 9.1).

### *Step 1*

Identify the presence and absence of the key indicators of a well-motivated team or department — i.e. good time-keeping, good attendance, good shop-floor housekeeping, supportive peer relationships, few grievances, good output, friendly competition, etc.

### *Step 2*

Implement the appropriate leadership skills — i.e. team building,

| Step 1 | Step 2 | Step 3 | Step 4 |
|---|---|---|---|
| Identify key motivation indicators | Implement appropriate leadership skills | Identify individual warning signals | Take appropriate corrective action |
| Good timekeeping<br><br>Good attendance<br><br>Good shopfloor housekeeping<br><br>Supportive peer relationships<br><br>Few grievances<br><br>Good output<br><br>Friendly competition | Teambuilding<br><br>Coaching<br><br>Problem-solving<br><br>Discipline handling<br><br>Planning<br><br>Organizing<br><br>Budgeting | Lack of interest in work<br><br>Resistance to overtime<br><br>Defensive attitude towards problems<br><br>Unwillingness to accept criticism<br><br>Lack of initiative | Counselling<br><br>Coaching<br><br>Incentives<br><br>Training |

*Figure 9.1. Leadership steps to a well-motivated team.*

empowering, coaching, problem-solving, discipline handling, planning, organizing, communicating, budgeting.

### *Step 3*

Monitor motivation levels and identify individual 'problem' areas by observation, discussion and counselling. Warning signals of poor motivation are lack of interest in work, resistance to overtime, defensive attitude towards problems, unwillingness to accept criticism, lack of initiative.

### *Step 4*

Take appropriate corrective action.

## Concern for the Workforce

### *Question: How is the impact of 'downsizing' softened?*

Most companies at some time are faced with the problem of making employees redundant. This is particularly true in times of recession, but redundancies occur also at other times, arising from industrial restructuring, the impact of new technology, relocation, or a change by the company to flatter organizational structures.

The handling of redundancy by employers has a significant effect on the morale of the employees remaining and on the public perception of the company. An example of massive bad publicity was seen with the government and British Coal's handling of pit closures in late 1992. So great was the uproar that the outcome was a suspension of action and an investigation by a Parliamentary Working Party into the proposed closures.

Before an employer declares redundancy there are a number of alternatives that can be considered, with compulsory redundancy as the very last option.

### *Natural wastage*

A freeze can be placed on recruitment and promotion in those areas where there is a real or projected surplus of staff. The complement of staff will be reduced when there are leavers who are not replaced.

### *Early retirement*

An analysis of company human resource statistics can identify the number of employees who are within five to 10 years of normal retirement. An early retirement package made up of an enhanced redundancy package and the payment of an early upgraded pension can prove attractive to many employees, particularly those with long service.

### *Short-time working*

An alternative to redundancy — and a means of retaining experienced employees — is to offer short-time working. The usual alternatives are to work part-time on a weekly basis or to adopt a pattern of one week on and one week off.

### *Redeployment*

In some cases employees can be considered for redeployment within the organization. This may involve retraining and/or relocation. The costs of relocation should be balanced against the costs that would have been incurred had the employee been made redundant. An example of this was seen in the massive upheaval of the newspaper industry in the early 1990s. Widespread retraining and relocation of printers was necessary following the introduction of new technology.

### *Voluntary redundancy*

The last step before declaring compulsory redundancies is to invite employees to apply for voluntary redundancy. The number of volunteers will depend on the generosity of the severance terms and the likelihood of finding alternative employment. If too many employees volunteer, companies have to devise selection criteria to decide who is allowed to leave.

A major drawback to voluntary redundancy is that often it is the best workers who apply for it is they who are most confident of finding other employment. In such circumstances the company may decline to release them and agree to the redundancy of less able employees. The outcome may be that voluntary redundancy is seen by some as a reward for poor performance and a certain demotivator.

## Fighting Back

### *Question: When mass redundancy is a reality, how is the change best managed?*

The crisis of change falls on the management and employees who remain after a redundancy purge: morale is rock-bottom. This crisis generally has four stages: personal shock, defensive resistance, acceptance of reality, and adaptive growth. Change can be managed positively provided that management resists hoping that the problem will go away by itself.

### *Personal shock*

How does shock manifest itself? One answer is disbelief. Other aspects are horror, hatred, worry, inability to think, feelings of weakness, a state of temporary speechlessness. Anger is another. For managers it is important that they are able to recognize shock and deal with it whenever it is present. Sometimes it is the manager himself or herself who has to start the change process.

Dealing with shock in others should be straightforward — through sympathy and encouragement. Sympathy and encouragement are human reactions that everyone can give naturally, without special training.

### *Defensive resistance*

Resistance is a complex matter. Employees and personnel caught up in the process of change resist that change. They are unwilling to adopt new ways of behaving. If it is possible to identify the mechanism of the resistance then there is an opportunity of helping management and staff to overcome it. The reasons for resistance include:

- Fear of the unknown
- Threat to individual skill
- Fear of failure
- Fear of looking stupid
- Lack of information
- Misinformation
- Threat to status
- Threat to power base
- No perceived benefits
- Climate of no trust
- Poor relationships
- Reluctance to let go
- Strong peer group norms.

Some causes of resistance to change are considerably easier to deal with than others. For example, a 'climate of no trust' may be a key issue but it is a much longer-term proposition than correcting misinformation. Resistance falls into two categories — behavioural and emotional. A threat to individual core skill is behavioural. Fear of looking stupid is emotional. The value of categorising is to identify which aspects of resistance are easier to correct and minimise than others.

Resistance to change will be overcome by influencing behaviour. Who to influence, and how, is best actioned by considering the players in the drama (See Figure 9.2). There are:

- Winners
- Losers
- Those who have power
- Those who have information — hard and soft.

Winners and losers are those who perceive that they will win or lose

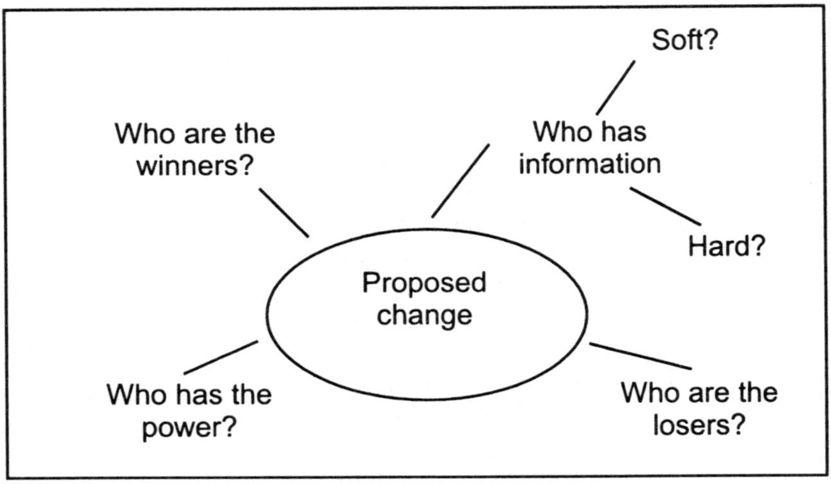


*Figure 9.2. Parties to the change process.*

from change. Winners and losers can also be whole departments: most organizations are a dynamic whole, made up of divisions or departments and subsections which move at their own different pace.

An example illustrates the concept of the loser in a change process. The setting is a change project in a company in the mining industry. The decision-making process through the various departments typically took 6—9 months. Each of the seven departments involved worked on their own aspect of the data. They then passed it up to their manager, who in turn passed it on to the next manager in the sequence, and so on. The 6—9 months needed for a decision was making the company uncompetitive in the market place, and a consultant was called in to devise and implement a better method of corporate decision-making. His solution was simple. He created a small project team drawn from each of the departments concerned and put them to work on the task. The result: an excellent quality decision in nine weeks. But the consultant had paid little attention to the departmental heads, apart from keeping them informed. He had assumed that they would bask in the reflected glory of the success story, but he was wrong. The managers saw themselves as losers because they had lost their control and their power base. The project worked only once and then reverted back to the original system for all sorts of good, sound reasons. Subsequently, some years later, the consultant's project system is working well within the company — but none of the original managers are still in their posts.

What is illustrated by this example is the failure to identify the needs of potential losers — and to adopt a strategy to turn losers into winners.

Those who have power in a company are those with the patronage that is needed for change, or are able to abort the process.

Those who have information are those informed about what exists now. Hard information includes data on stocks, products, prices, manpower levels and the like. Soft information is 'How does one approach Mr Brown about sensitive areas in his department?' or 'How reliable and competent is Mr Smith?' Access to both types of information is crucial to the management of change. But equally important is the giving of up-to-date information about the change and how it is being implemented. Everyone who is in a position to disseminate positive information has to be used. When the parties to the change process, as described above, are identified the influence of persuasion must be exerted. Persuasion is three-pronged:

- Empathy
- Communication
- Counselling.

### *Empathy*

Empathy is putting oneself in the position of the other person. A parent watching her child doing the high jump at a school sports day may lift her leg as the child goes over the bar. That is empathy, and it also applies to the workforce: managers can work at predicting how staff are likely to react to change.

The first step in the exercise is the preparation of 'checklist No.1'. Professor Kirkpatrick, a former President of the Society for Training and Development in the USA, argues that empathy is not an inherited trait: it is something that can be developed in a systematic way, by getting to know the other person. He calls the first checklist the *know factor* list. It is a practical tool for getting to know the most important things.

For each employee or supervisor a list is made up of everything that can be thought of about the individual — e.g. name, nickname, home, whether home is owned or rented, status, etc. On the right-hand side of the checklist are three columns: very important/important/ unimportant. A tick is put in one of the three columns relating to the importance or otherwise of the item.

The next step is to prepare the *Empathy worksheet*. The items ticked as 'very important' in the first checklist are entered across the top of another grid document. Each of the 'very important' known factor items is given a vertical column. On each horizontal line the name of a member of staff is entered. The question is then asked: 'Do I know this about the individual?' If 'Yes' an X is put in the appropriate square — otherwise it is left blank. Analysis of the completed form will clearly indicate the important factors that are known and those for which information still has to be sought.

The third grid Kirkpatrick calls the *Empathy regarding change* form. Before talking about change and before counselling individual staff, the manager makes a judgement about the position of the person on a scale of 'Resists: Resents: Neutral: Accepts: Welcomes: Not Sure'. The more accurate the judgement is through this derived knowledge of the person, the easier it is to plan and implement change.

### *Communication*

Communication is the two-way process of transmitting and receiving messages and signals. It is one of the key areas in the management of change. But the process of communication is not always smooth; there are barriers. There are sender barriers and receiver barriers as well as barriers due to the medium by which messages are communicated.

Examples of sender barriers are:

- The sender doesn't know enough about the receiver.
- The sender doesn't like the message.
- The sender doesn't like the receiver.
- The sender has poor communication skills.
- The sender chooses the wrong place or time.
- The sender is in a hurry.

Examples of receiver barriers are:

- The receiver is preoccupied.
- The receiver doesn't like or respect the sender.
- The receiver is physically tired.
- The receiver is distracted.
- The receiver doesn't want to understand the message.
- The receiver only pretends to listen.

Being aware of the barriers to communication is the first step in overcoming them. But there is another type of hurdle the communication process has to surmount in the management of change.

We are trained at school and college and work to think sequentially. First comes planning: then comes implementation. In communication terms this is the 'what' and the 'how'. 'What' is the logistical alteration and change. 'How' is the way in which change is introduced. In successful management of change 'how' and 'what' must be activated together — in parallel. But this is often difficult. Experience — and literature on the management of change — show that whilst the concept of parallel implementation is understandable on an intellectual level, it is very difficult for managers to put it into practice. It seems to go against the logic of how we behave.

There is a classroom exercise that illustrates this point. Two groups are formed — one of planners and one of implementers. The planners have to work out how to instruct the implementing team to carry out a fairly complex assembly task. The planners must not do any of the assembly themselves. They must simply draw up a plan for the implementers to carry out.

The planners are put in one room; the implementers are put in another room and told to organize and occupy themselves as best they can. Neither group has any constraints on contact with the other team. In almost every case, the two groups do not meet within the time allowed for the exercise. If they do, it is always at the instigation of the implementers — who then receive short shrift from the busy planners who are engrossed in their tasks.

When the planners finally deliver the results of their hard work to the implementing group they usually encounter reactions that range from lack of interest to obstruction. Frequently, in industry, senior management beaver away on a difficult long-term plan without discussing it with other managers. The reason is that 'We don't have anything final or sensible to say yet'. By the time the plan is ready, it is too late. Change has to be talked about before it becomes change.

A real-life example of this was recently written up in a management journal. Senior management of a company decided that they could help the workforce achieve greater output by upgrading the machinery. They researched thoroughly, and bought a new machine incorporating many improvements. Particularly attractive was the great reduction in operator stress. As a reward for consistently good performance they decided to give the initial machine to a particular worker.

Over the weekend the old machine was taken away and the new one installed. This was a real surprise for the worker concerned. On the Monday morning when he arrived for work and was confronted with the change, management made a big fuss — because you have worked diligently we are installing this great new machine: it is easier for you to operate and everyone is going to benefit.

Management was disappointed to find that over the next months the machine did not live up to the manufacturer's promises. There was much downtime, and many short runs. With hindsight, management realized that it was worker malfunction, not machine malfunction, that was the problem. And the fault was theirs: management of change was not practised effectively.

### *Counselling*

Counselling is the third and final prong of persuasion. There are two types of counselling in the climate of redundancy: welfare counselling to improve the morale of those made redundant and to manage those who have to decide on the redundancies; and outplacement counselling to help redundant employees market themselves effectively.

*Welfare counselling.* For employees made redundant the effect is traumatic. Many will feel ashamed. It is not unknown for some employees to hide from their family the fact that they have lost their job. Welfare counselling should be provided by experienced personnel and outside assistance may be required.

Counselling interviews must be completely confidential. Redundant staff should be made aware of the availability of a counselling service, and counsellors are given the names of the redundant staff. Counselling is usually carried out on company premises in company time, but in some cases counselling may need to be carried out at the employee's home. The service should be made available to ex-employees for as long as the counsellor thinks appropriate.

*Outplacement counselling.* The purpose of outplacement counselling is to help those made redundant market themselves and find other employment. The form of outplacement counselling will depend on the level of the redundant employee and the cost to the company in providing the service. In some large organizations this service is provided in-house; for others external organizations are used.

For senior management outplacement counselling takes the form of a series of one-to-one interviews with psychometric testing to identify the employee's strengths, weaknesses and most marketable characteristics. Assistance will also be given in writing a curriculum vitae and in interview techniques. Often facilities are made available in the form of a desk, telephone, and secretarial services to help in the job search. For more junior personnel counselling sessions operate on a group basis, with training provided in writing CVs and interview skills.

Employers can and should do everything possible to assist redundant employees find work. One of the most successful ways is for organizations to contact local employers, company suppliers and customers, advising them of the skills available. Contact should also be made with local job centres and press advertisements should regularly be scanned for suitable vacancies for the company's redundant staff.

Federal Express, when shutting down its UK operation with the loss of 3,500 jobs in 1991, advertised in national newspapers inviting other employers to make contact. Considerable interest was generated and approximately 800 vacancies were notified to the company.

## Summary

*Question:* What management homework precedes effective motivation?

*Answer:* Before the introduction of any motivation scheme management must identify clearly what and how employees think. Information can be gathered by conducting regular attitude surveys.

*Question:* How effective are suggestion schemes?

*Answer:* Suggestion schemes generally produce a range of benefits, including increased profitabilty, cost savings, increased safety and boosts to morale. The schemes also act as indicators of employee mood.

*Question:* What suggestion scheme format creates the best opportunities for savings and improvement?

*Answer:* The criteria for the suggestion scheme is that (1) the change could not be made on the employee's own responsibility and (2) the absence of change does not make the employee liable to criticism by management. Companies are advised to devise rewards for suggestions and to operate a company-wide suggestions scheme through a Suggestions Scheme Committee.

*Question:* What are the motivational aspects of teamwork?

*Answer:* A small team working together with flexible competences, job rotation and with empowerment for self-organization maintains high work quality and high production. A high level of job satisfaction results.

*Question:* What role does team briefing play in teamwork?
*Answer:* Team briefing is a regular means of keeping employees informed of company performance, successes and future plans. It offers the stabilizing influence of reliable information.

*Question:* How do leadership skills influence motivation?
*Answer:* There is a structure to the leadership of a well motivated team, made up of four discrete steps:

1. Identify the key indicators of a well-motivated team.
2. Implement appropriate leadership skills.
3. Monitor individual 'problem' areas.
4. Take appropriate corrective action through counselling, coaching, incentives and training.

*Question:* How is the impact of 'downsizing' softened?
*Answer:* There are a number of options open to management to soften the requirement to shed staff. They are:

1. Natural wastage
2. Early retirement
3. Short-time working
4. Redeployment
5. Voluntary redundancy.

*Question:* When mass redundancy is a reality, how is the change best managed?
*Answer:* The crisis of change has to deal with four stages: personal shock, defensive resistance, acceptance of reality and adaptive growth. The major tool is the influence of persuasion exerted through positive empathy, effective communication and welfare and outplacement counselling.

# Further Reading


Adler, P. S. *Time and Motion Regained,* Harvard Business Review, Jan/Feb 1993.

Bower, A.M. and Lupton, T., *Handbook of Salary and Wage Systems,* Gower, 1990.

Carlzon, J., *Moments of Truth,* Harper & Row, 1989.

Fletcher, S., *NVQ's Standards and Competence,* Kogan Page, 1991.

Harrison, R., *Training and Development,* IPM, 1988.

Katz, B., *How to Manage Customer Service,* Gower, 1987.

Katz, B., *Turning Practical Communication into Business Power,* Management Books 2000, 1989.

Lock, D. and Farrow, N., *Handbook of Management,* Gower, 1988.

McDonald, R., *Motivative Skills,* Human Resource Development Press, 1985.

Peters, T., *Thriving on Chaos,* Guild Publishing Ltd, 1988.

Reid M., Barringon H. and Kenney J., *Training Interventions,* IPM, 1992.

Thomason, G., *A Textbook of Human Resource Management,* IPM, 1988.

Ungerson, B., *How to Write a Job Description,* IPM, 1983.

White, G., *Effective and Satisfactory Work Systems,* ACAS Research Unit Occasional Paper, 1983.

White, G., *Employee Commitment,* ACAS Research Unit, Advisory Booklet No. 2, 1991; Booklet Nos. 13, 17, 1992.


*(See also books listed on page 196)*

# Index